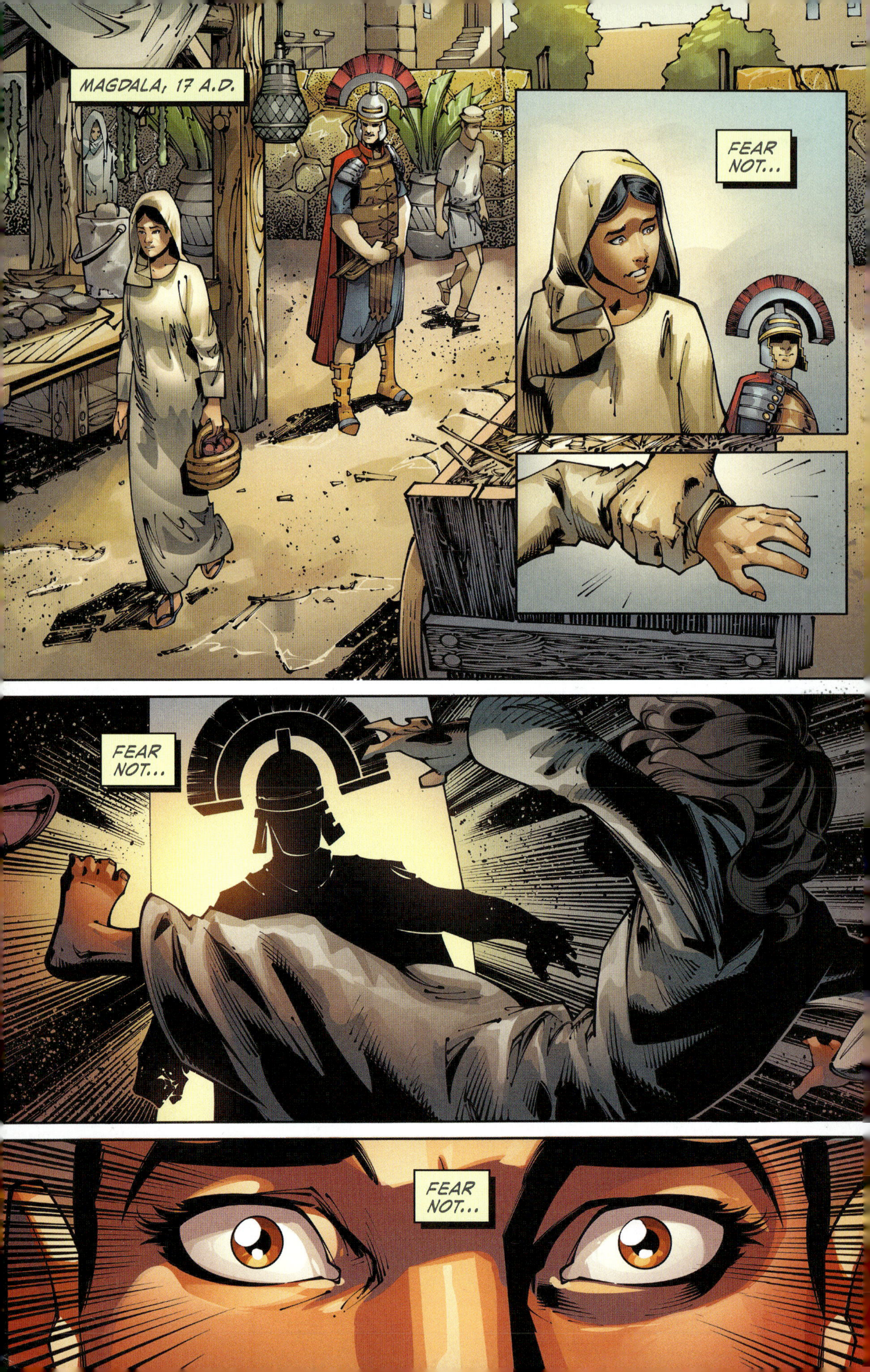

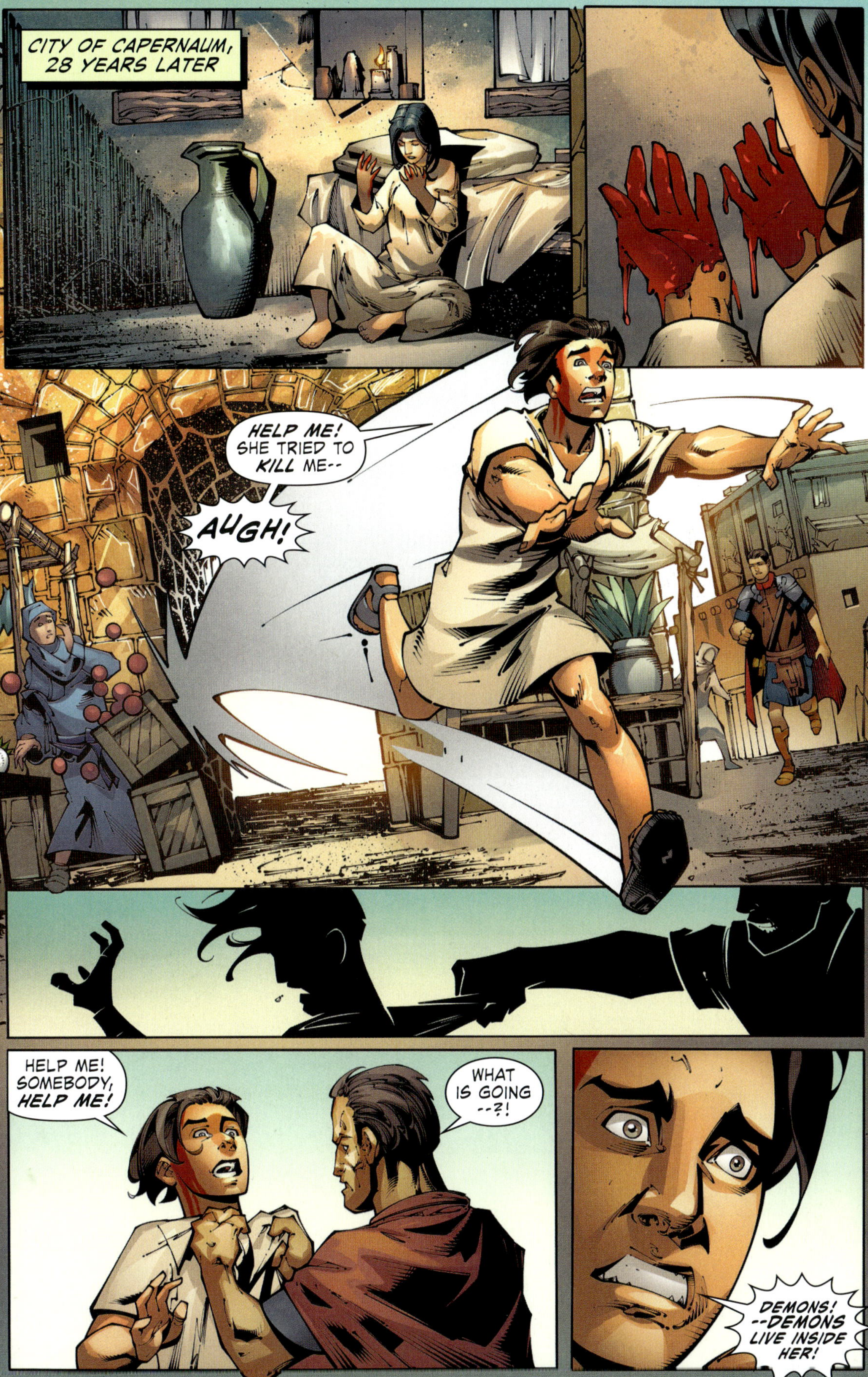

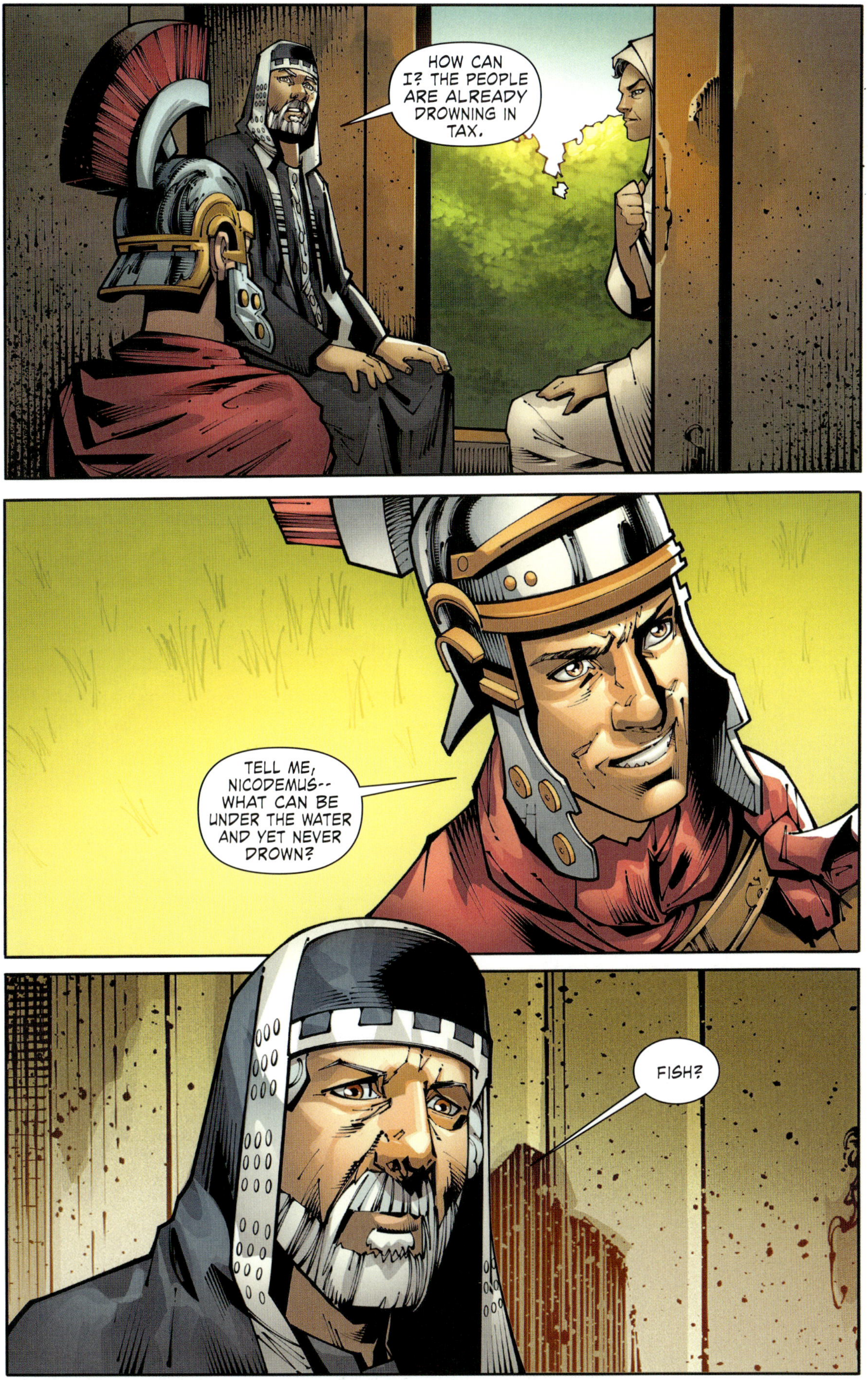

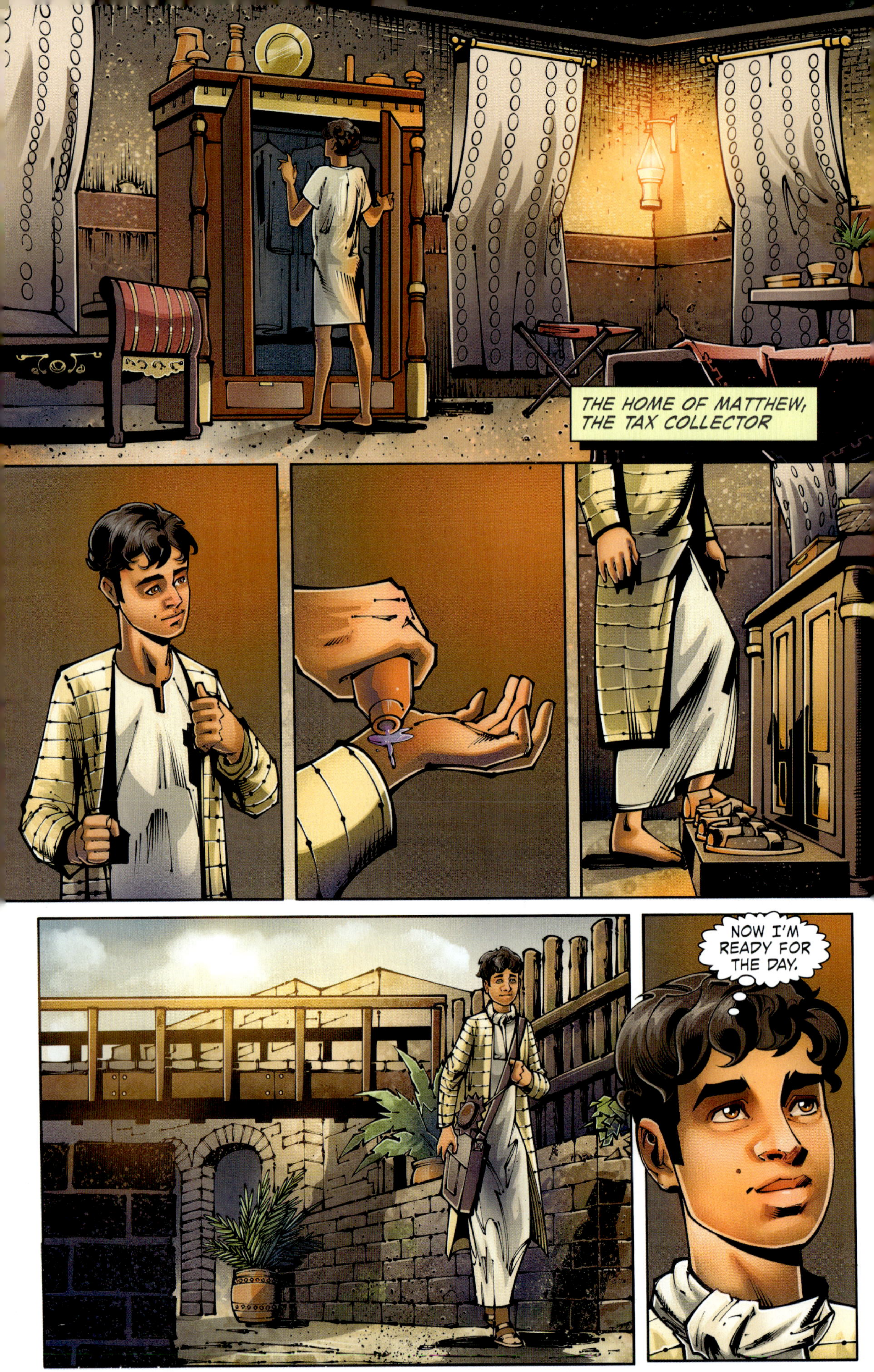

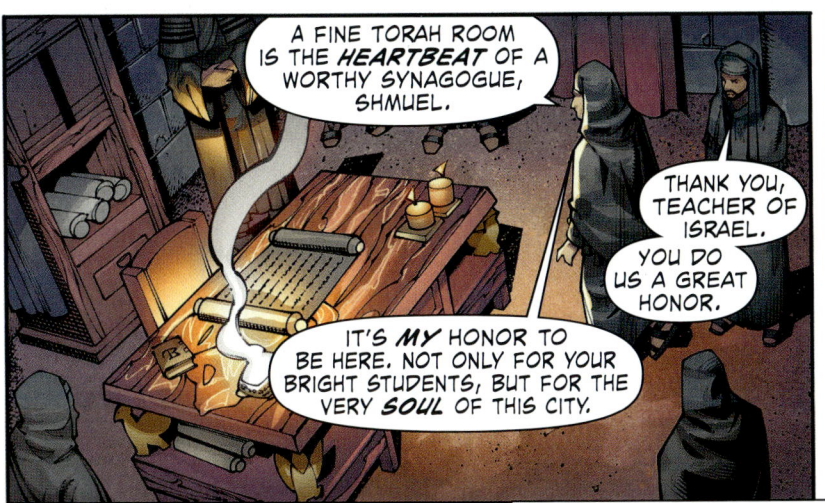

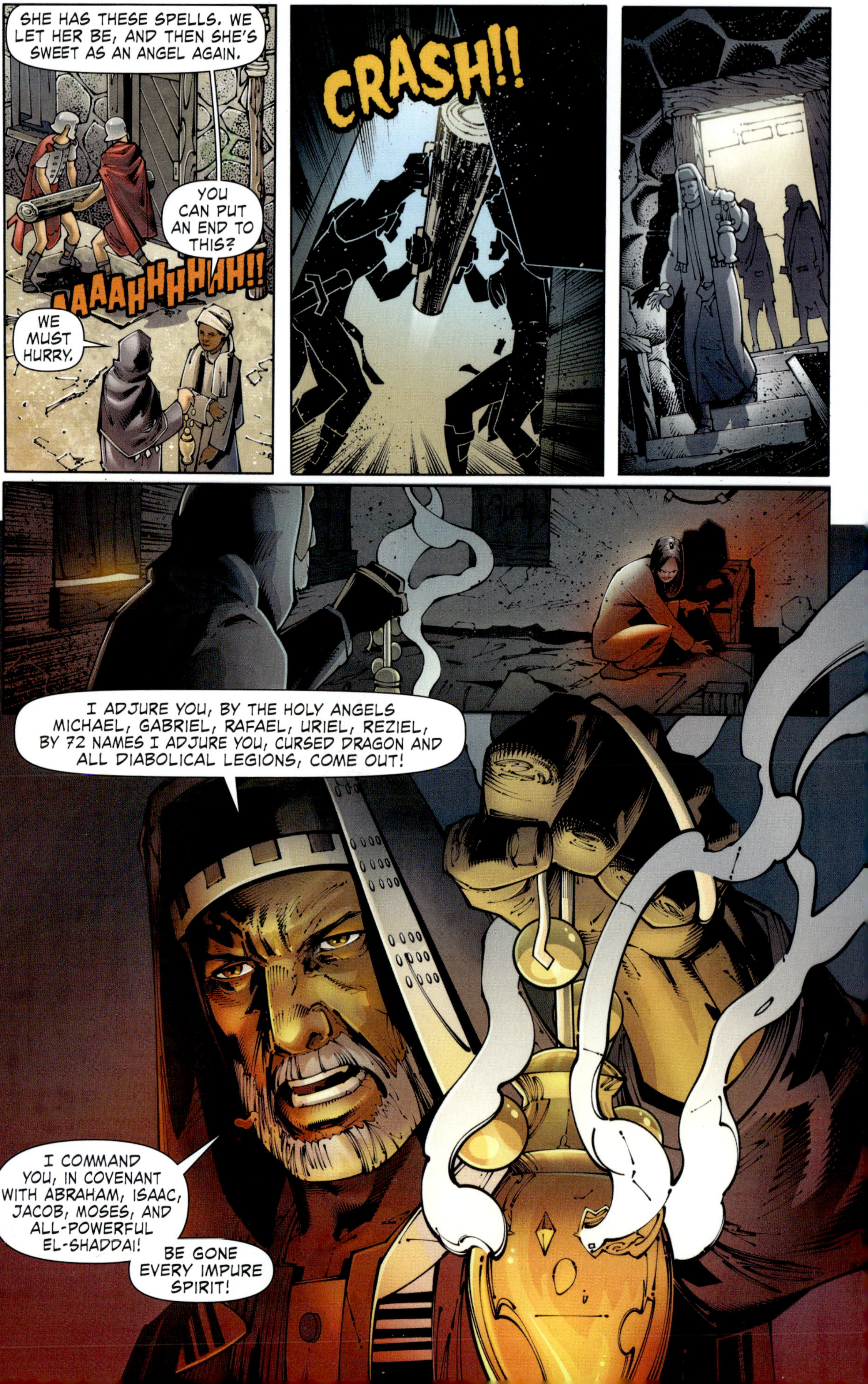

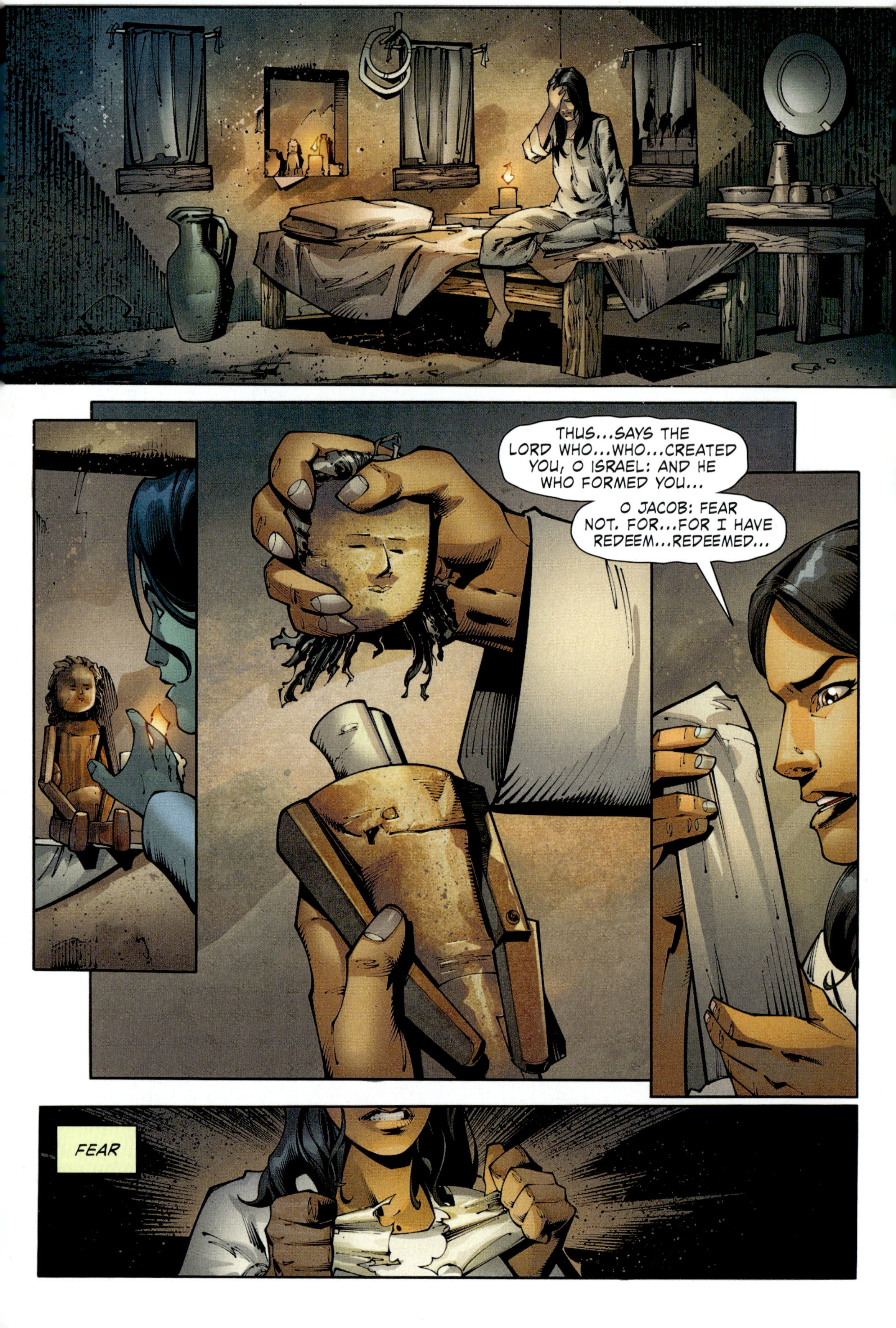

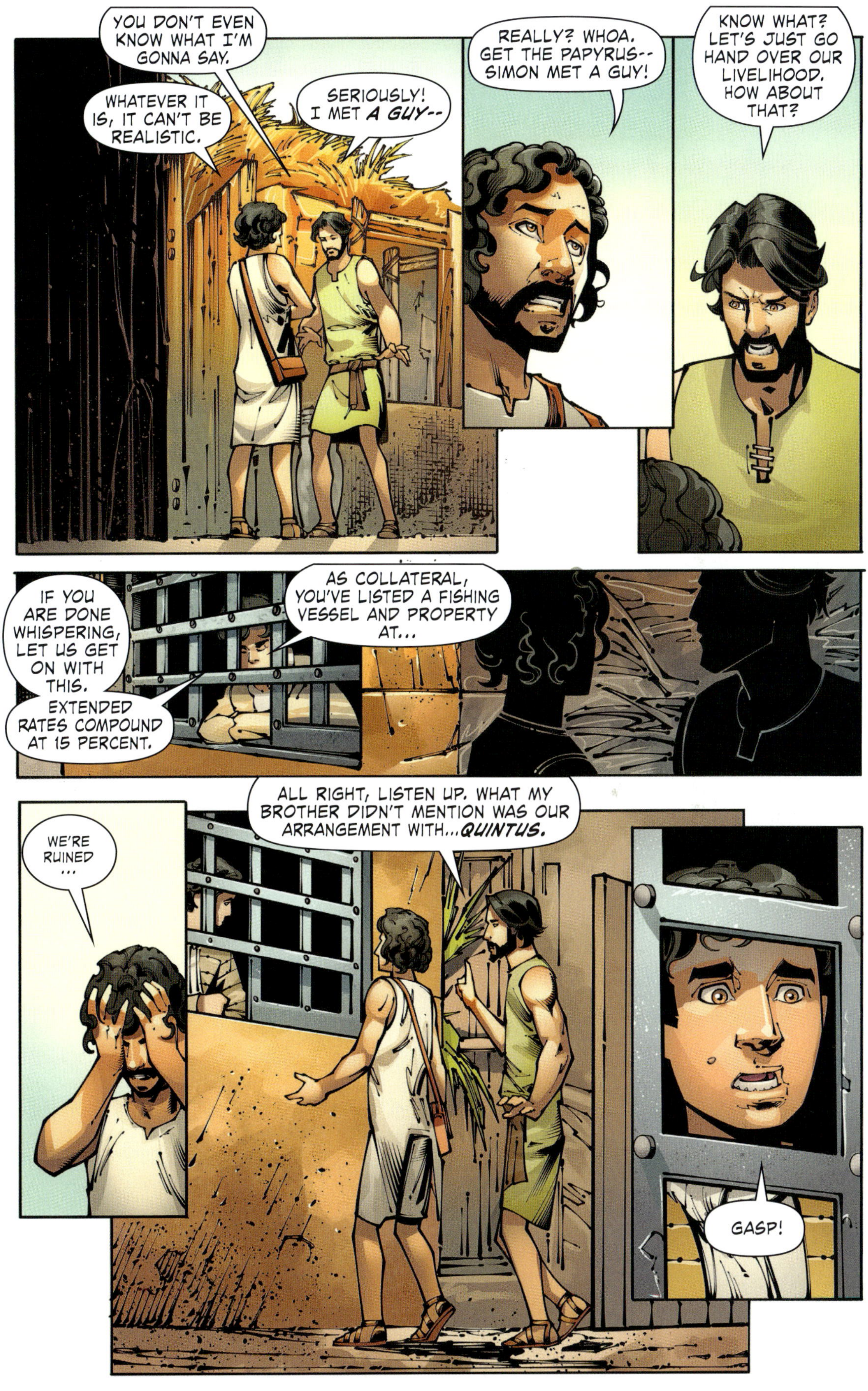

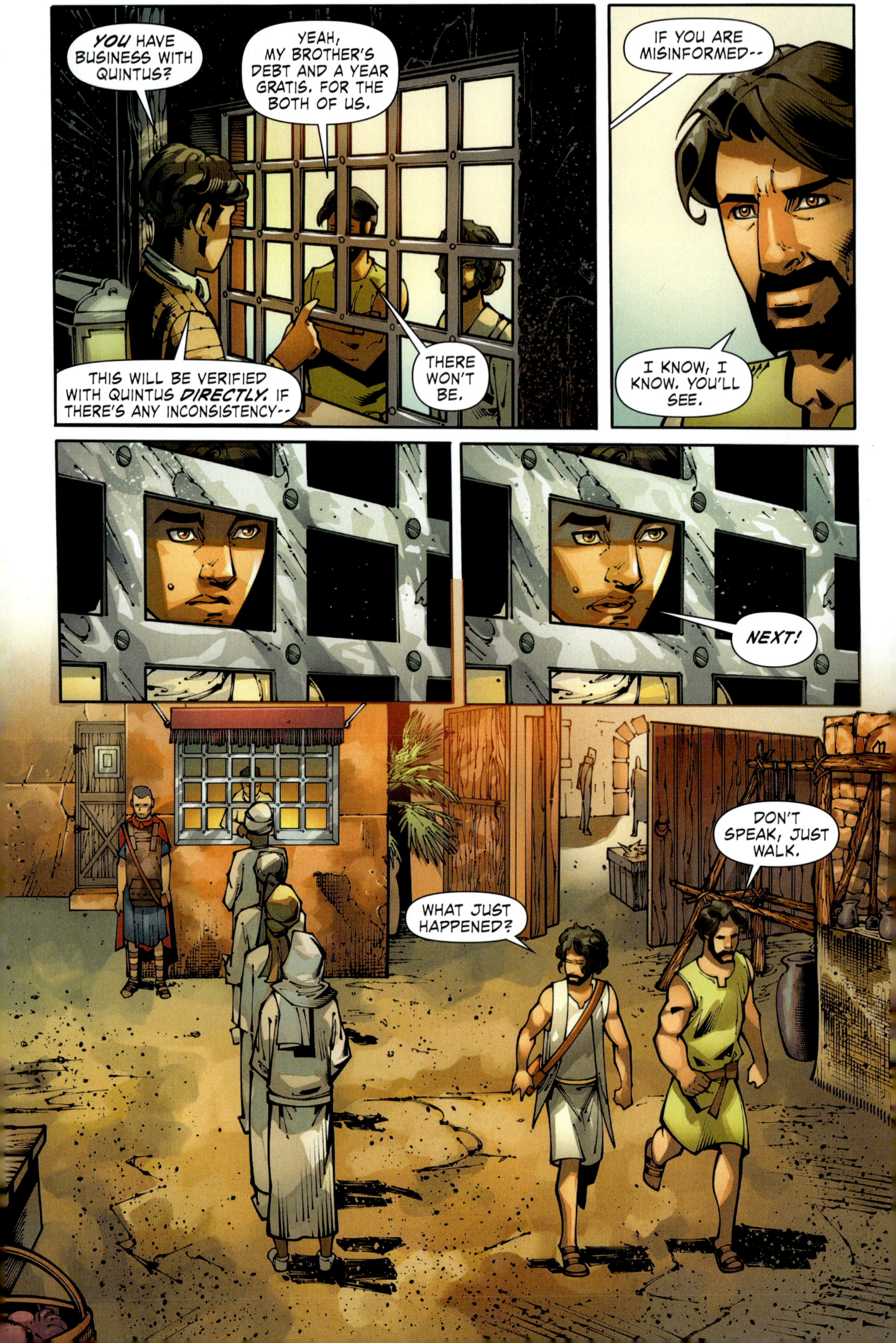

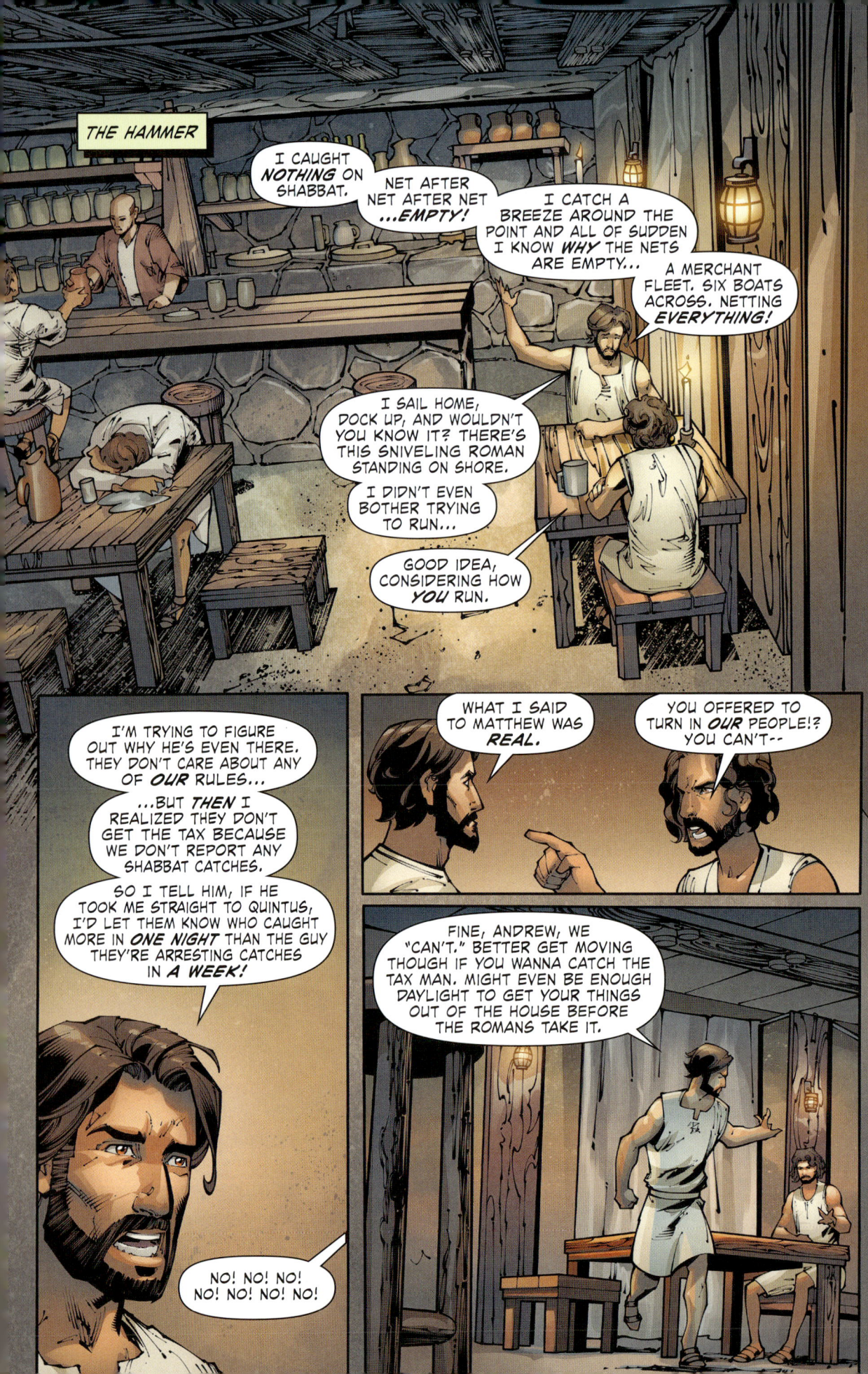

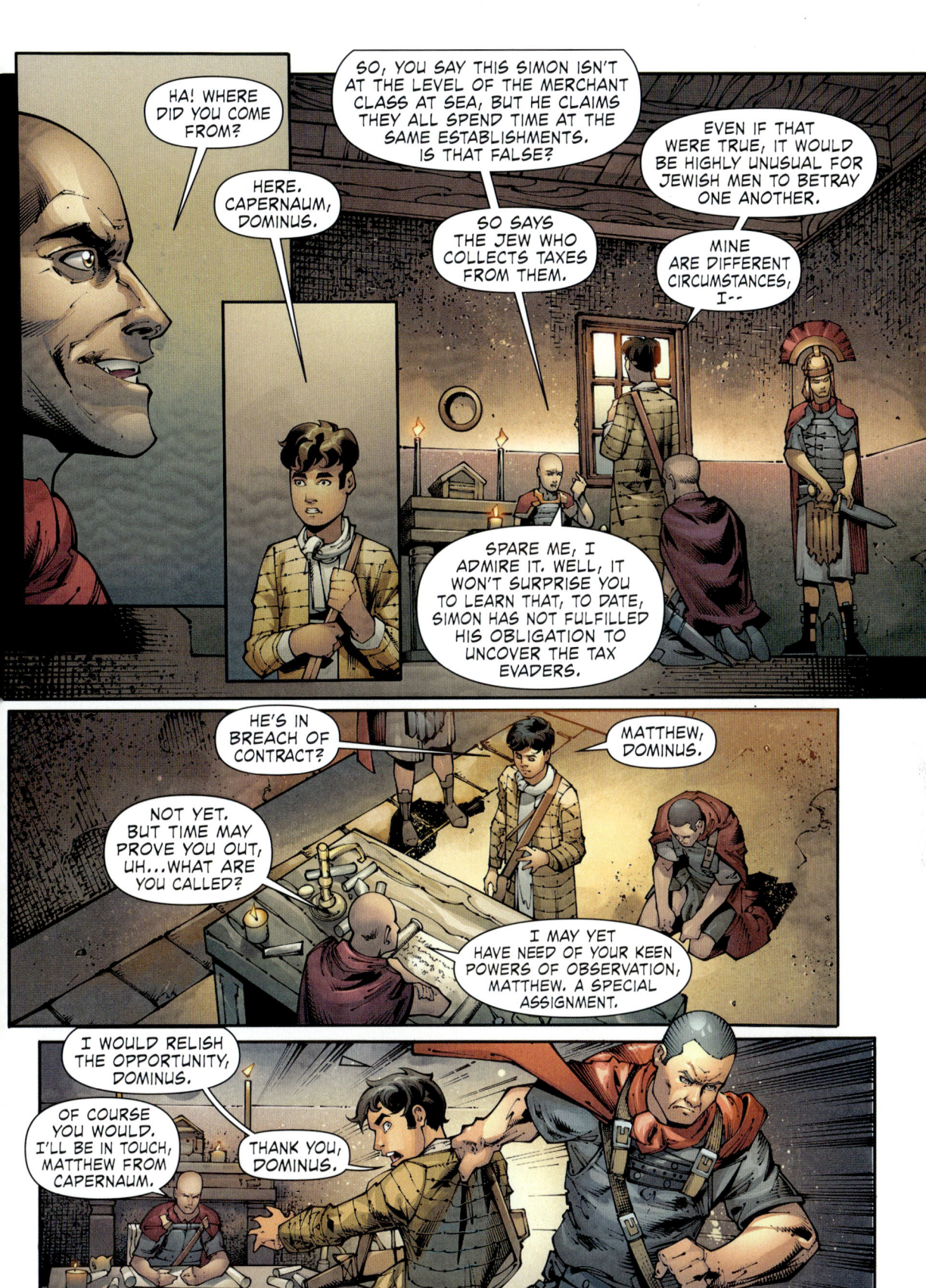

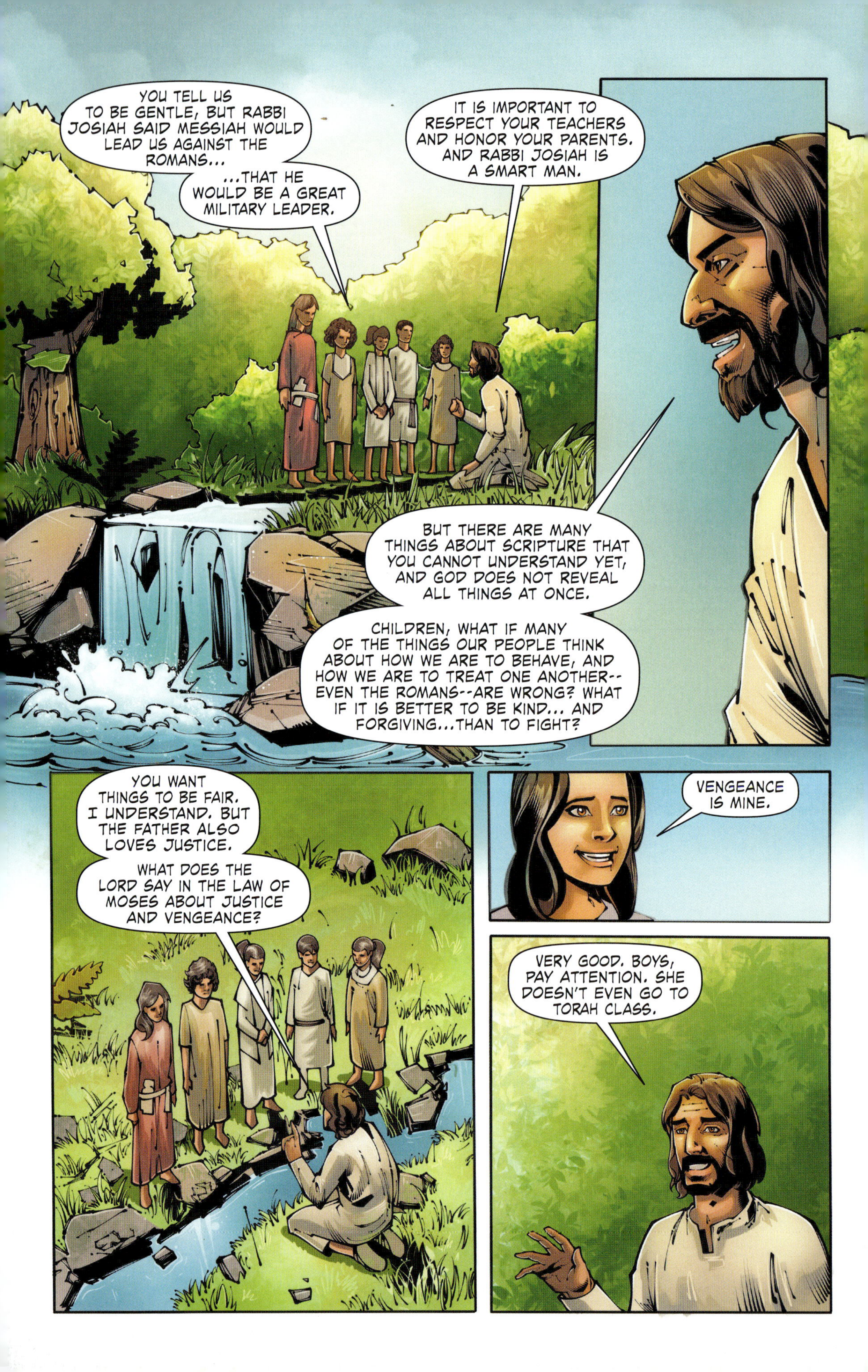

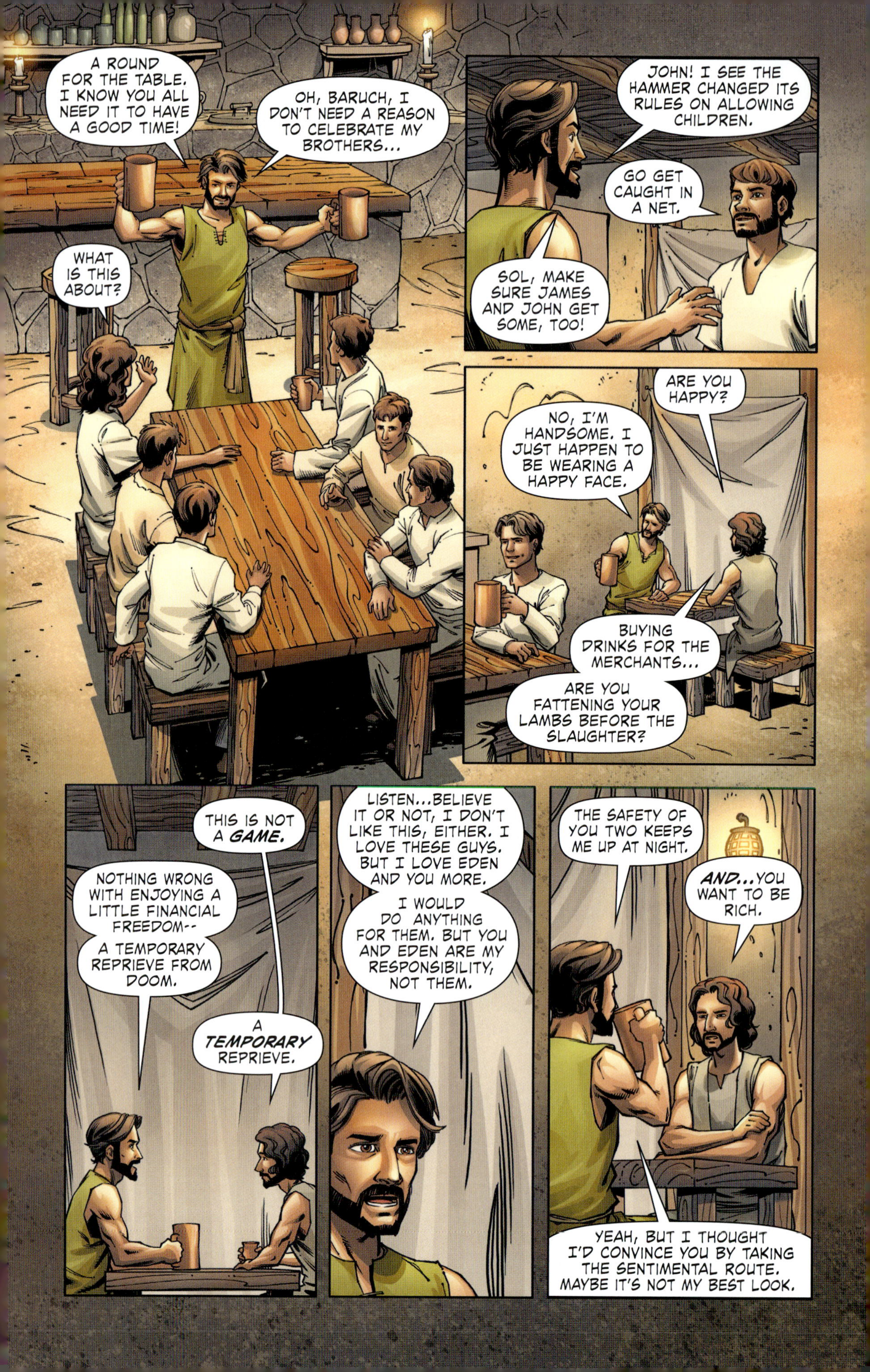

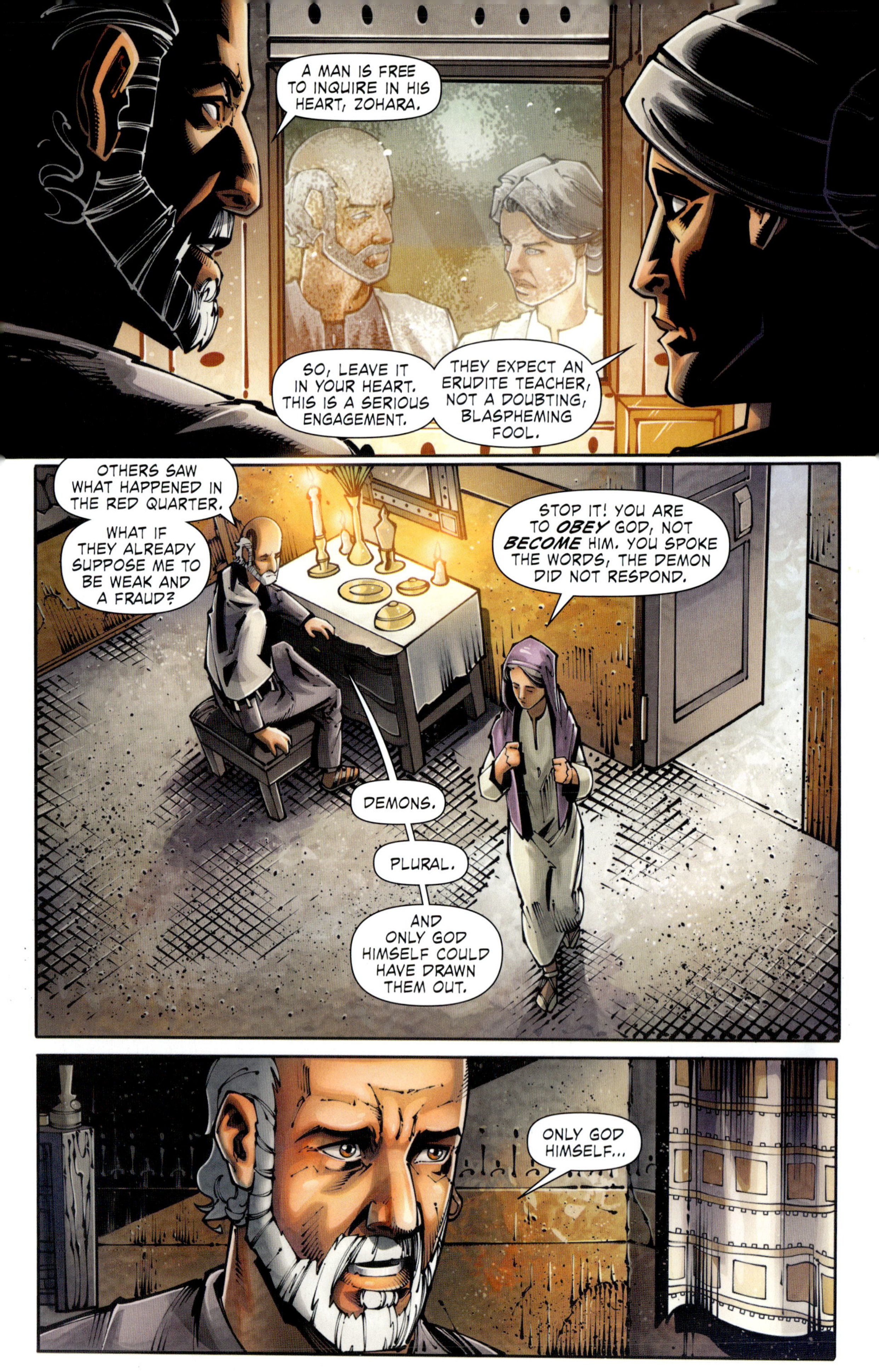

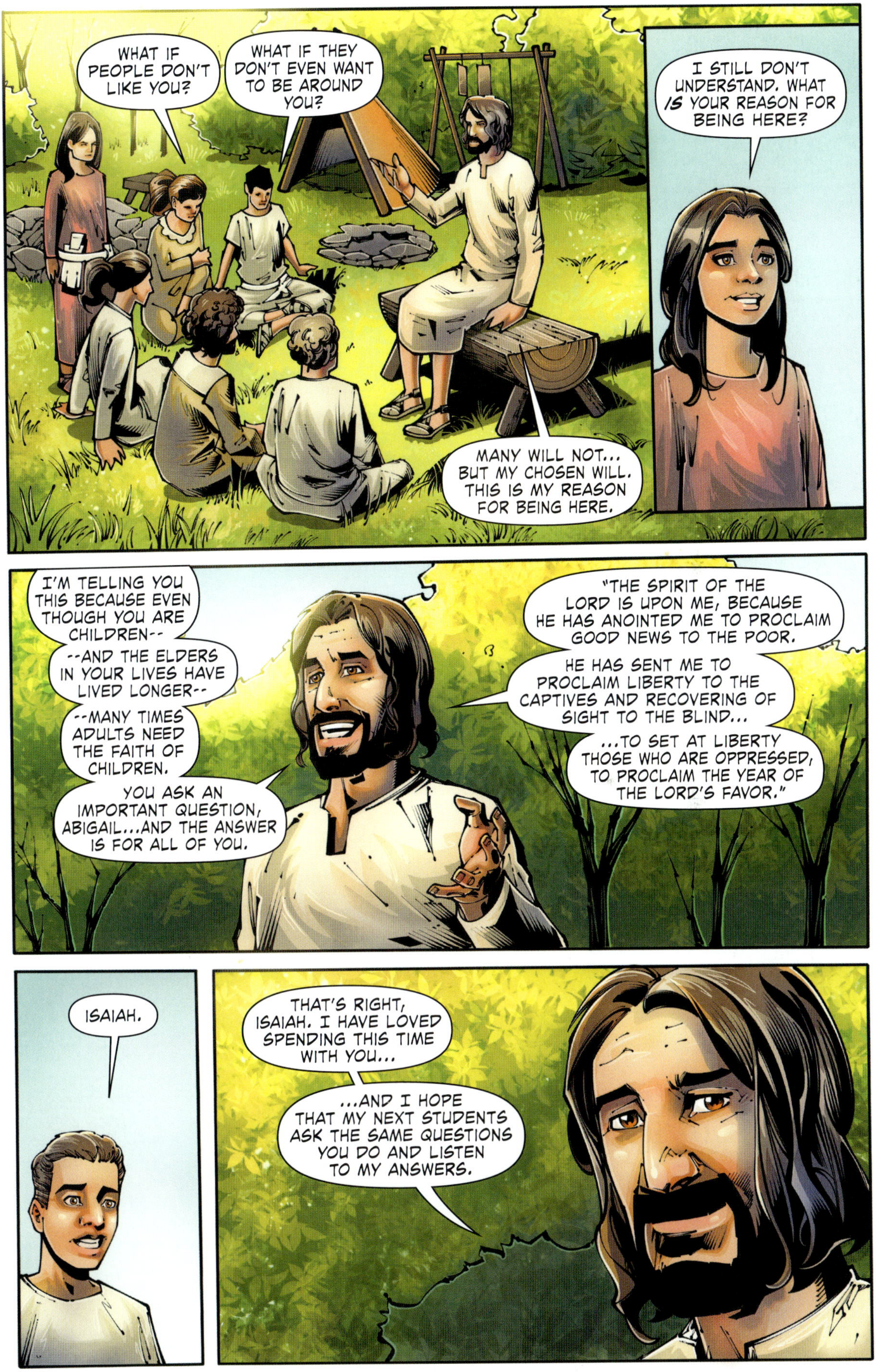

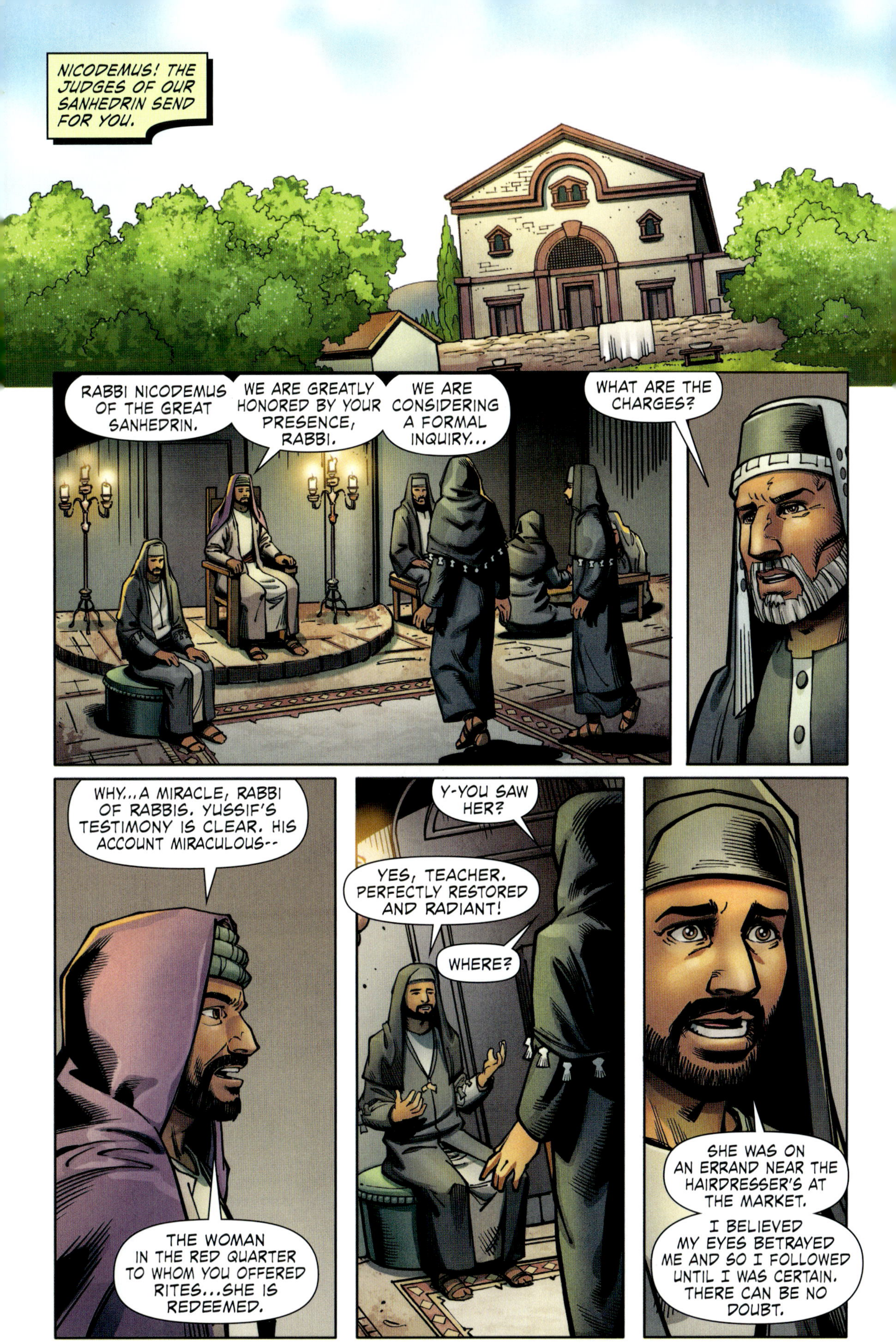

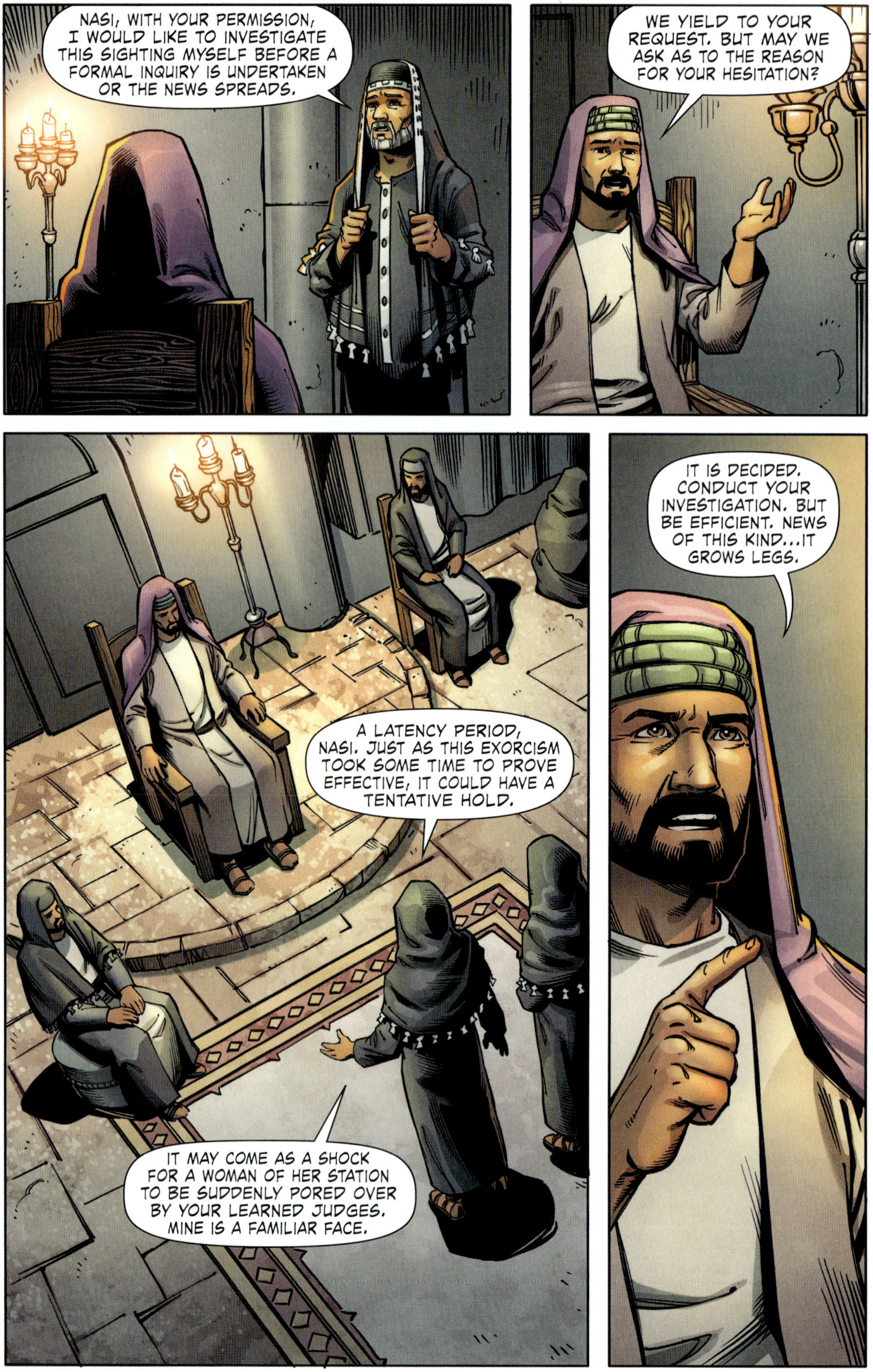

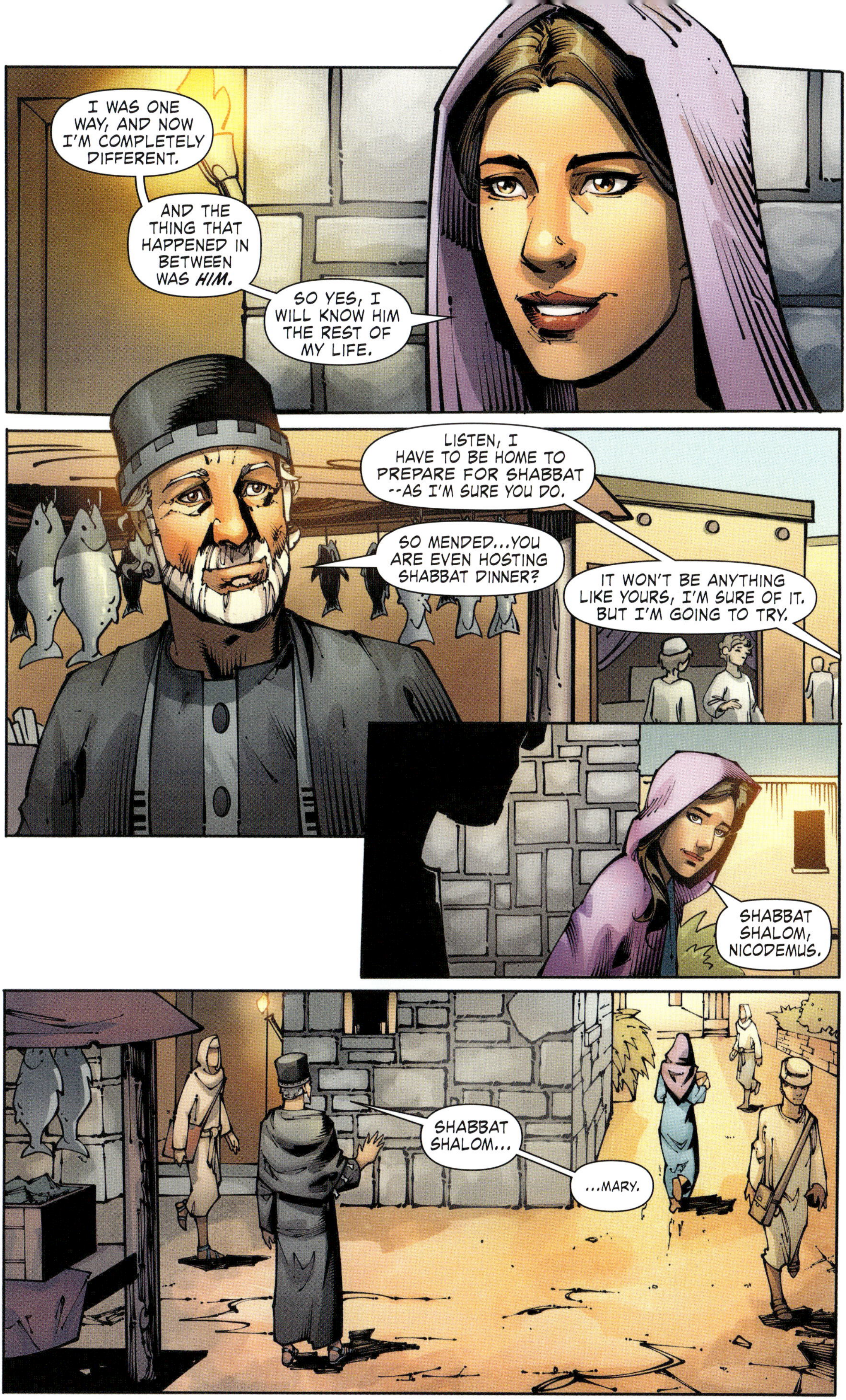

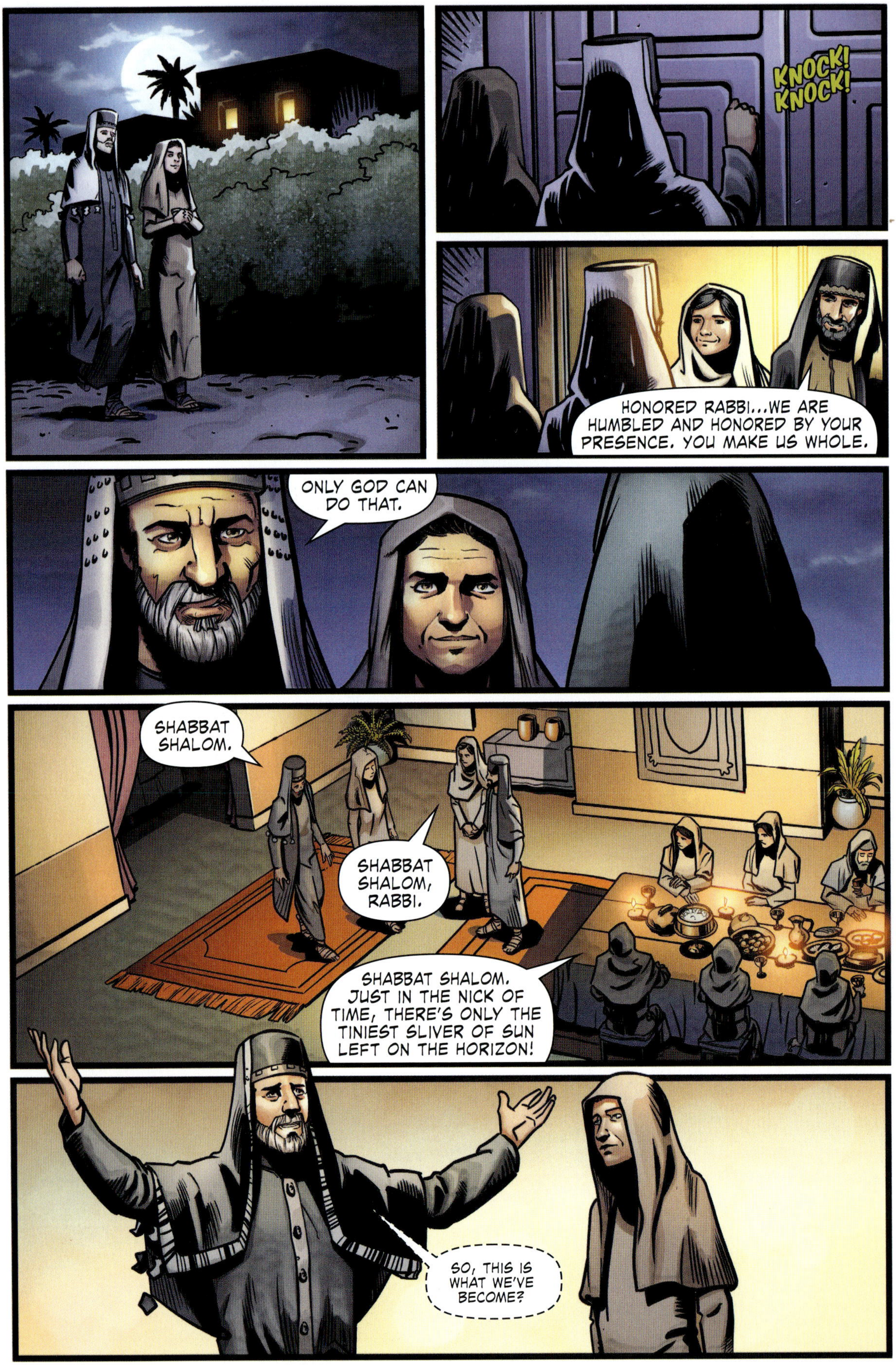

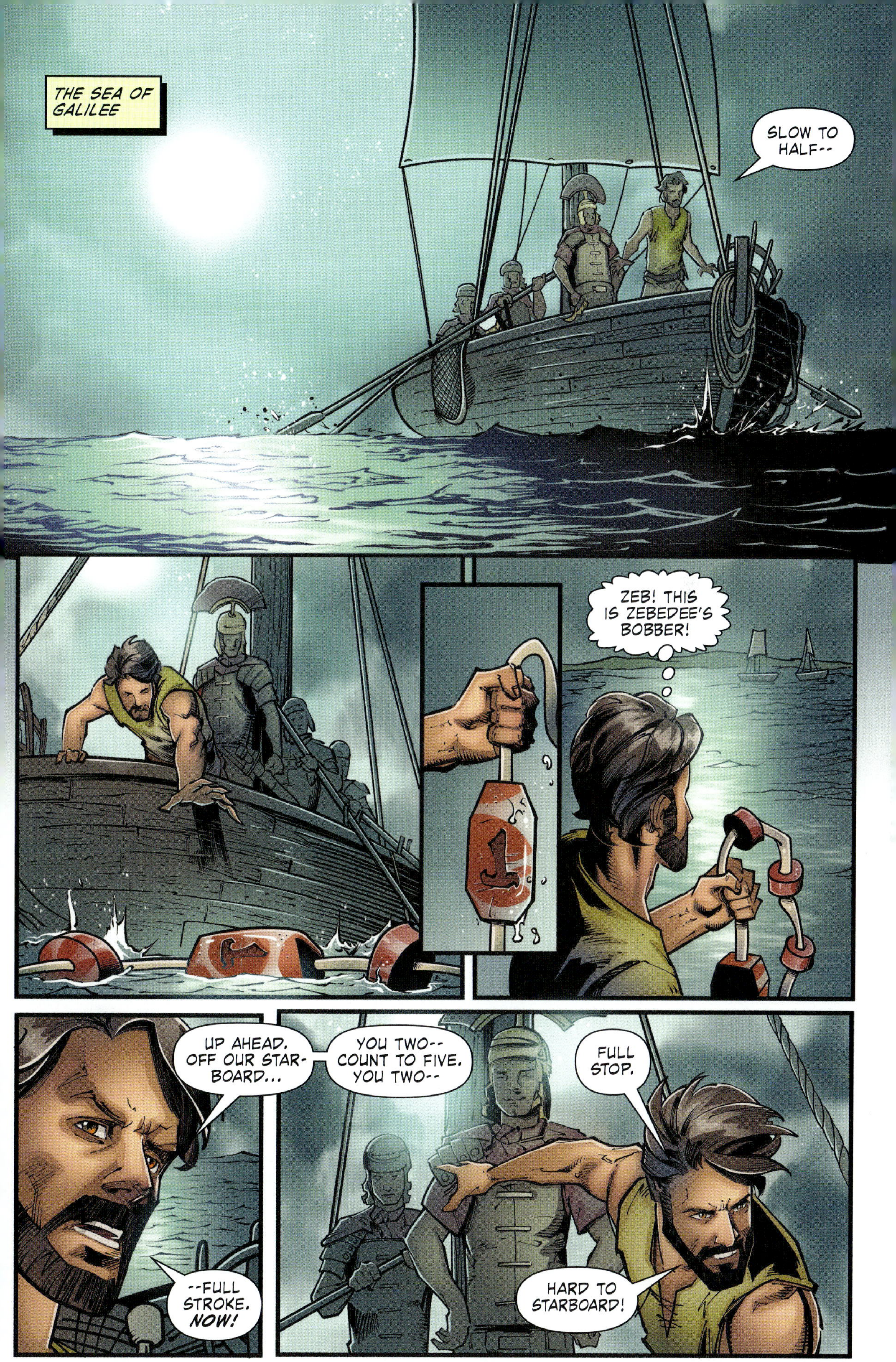

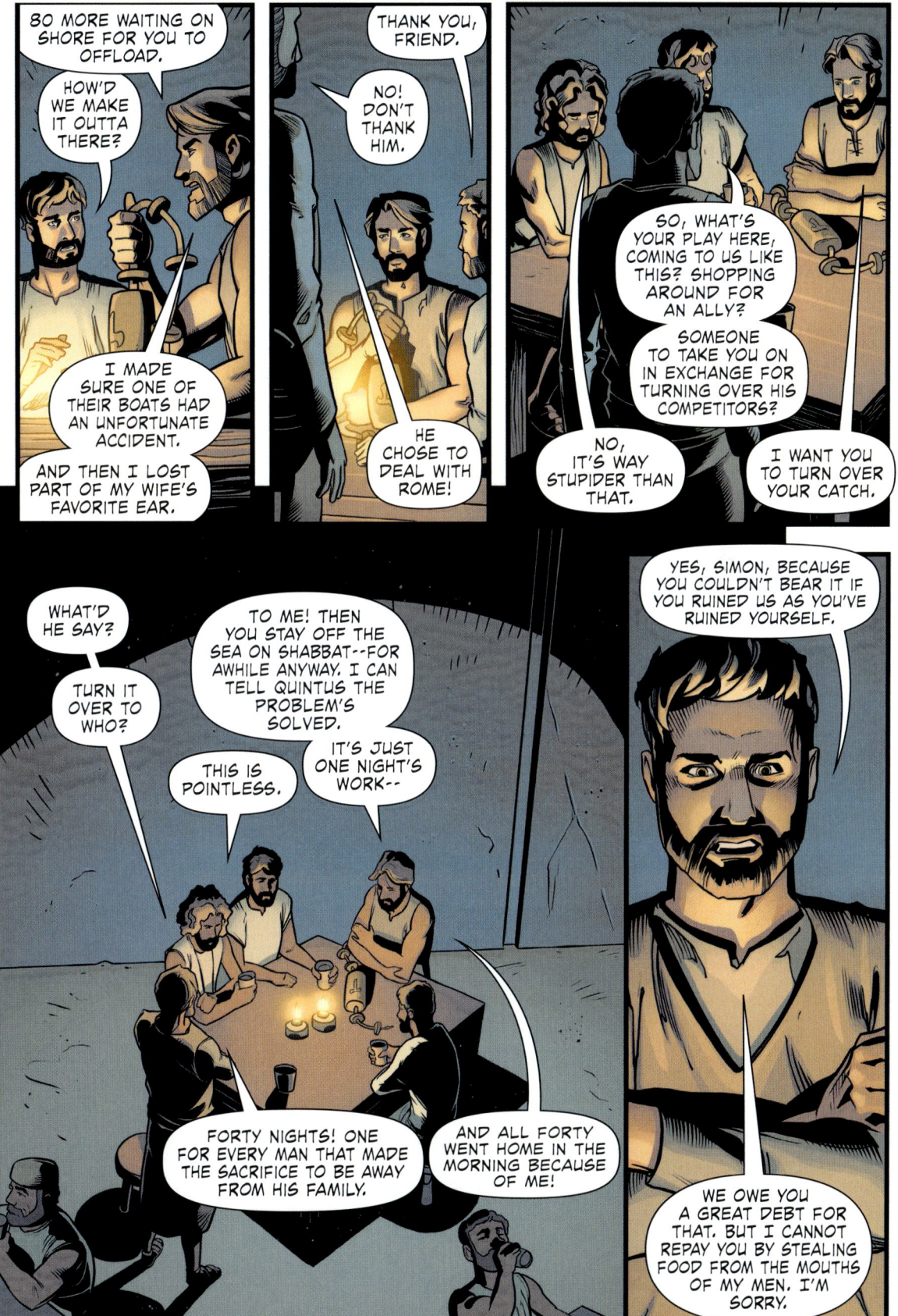

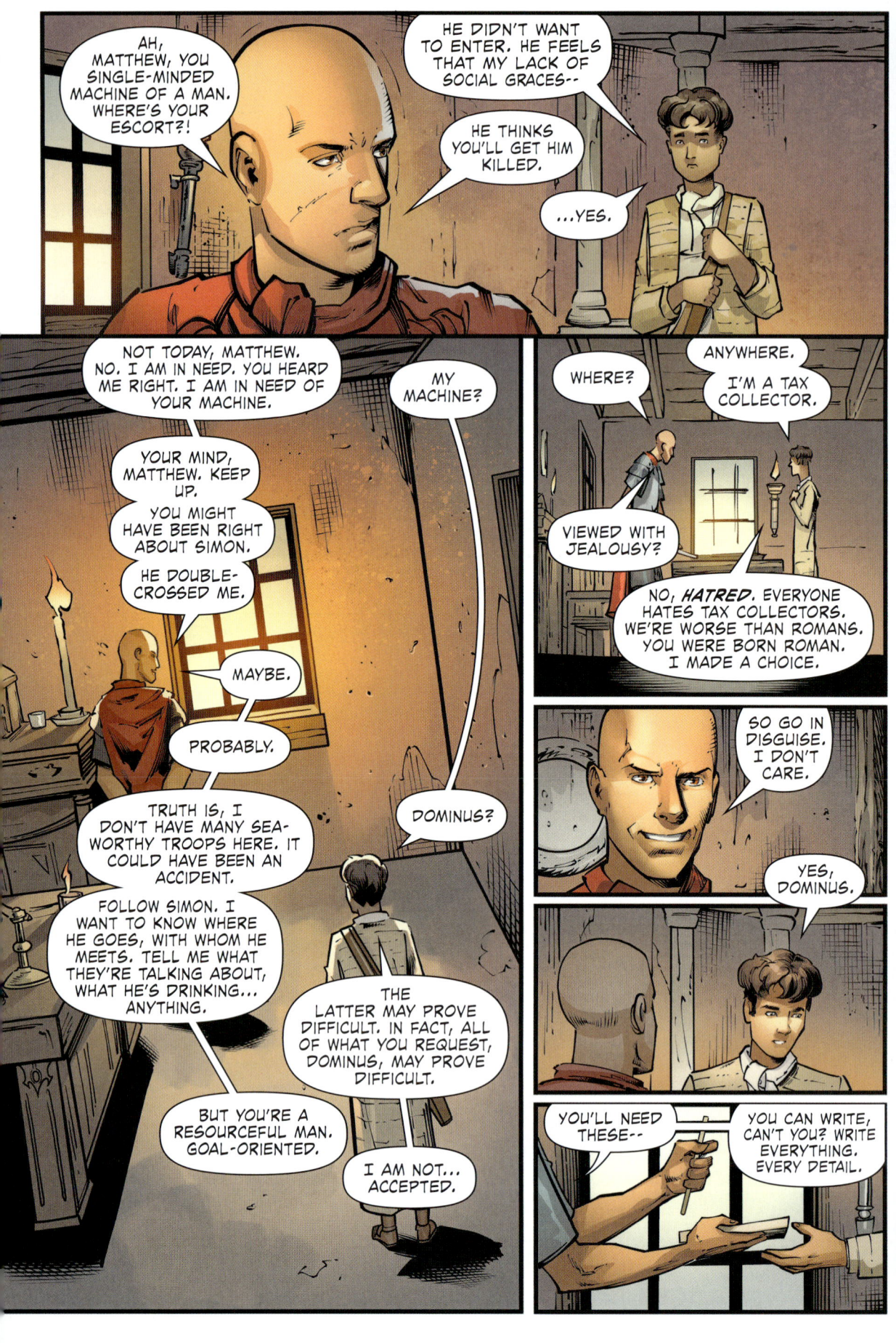

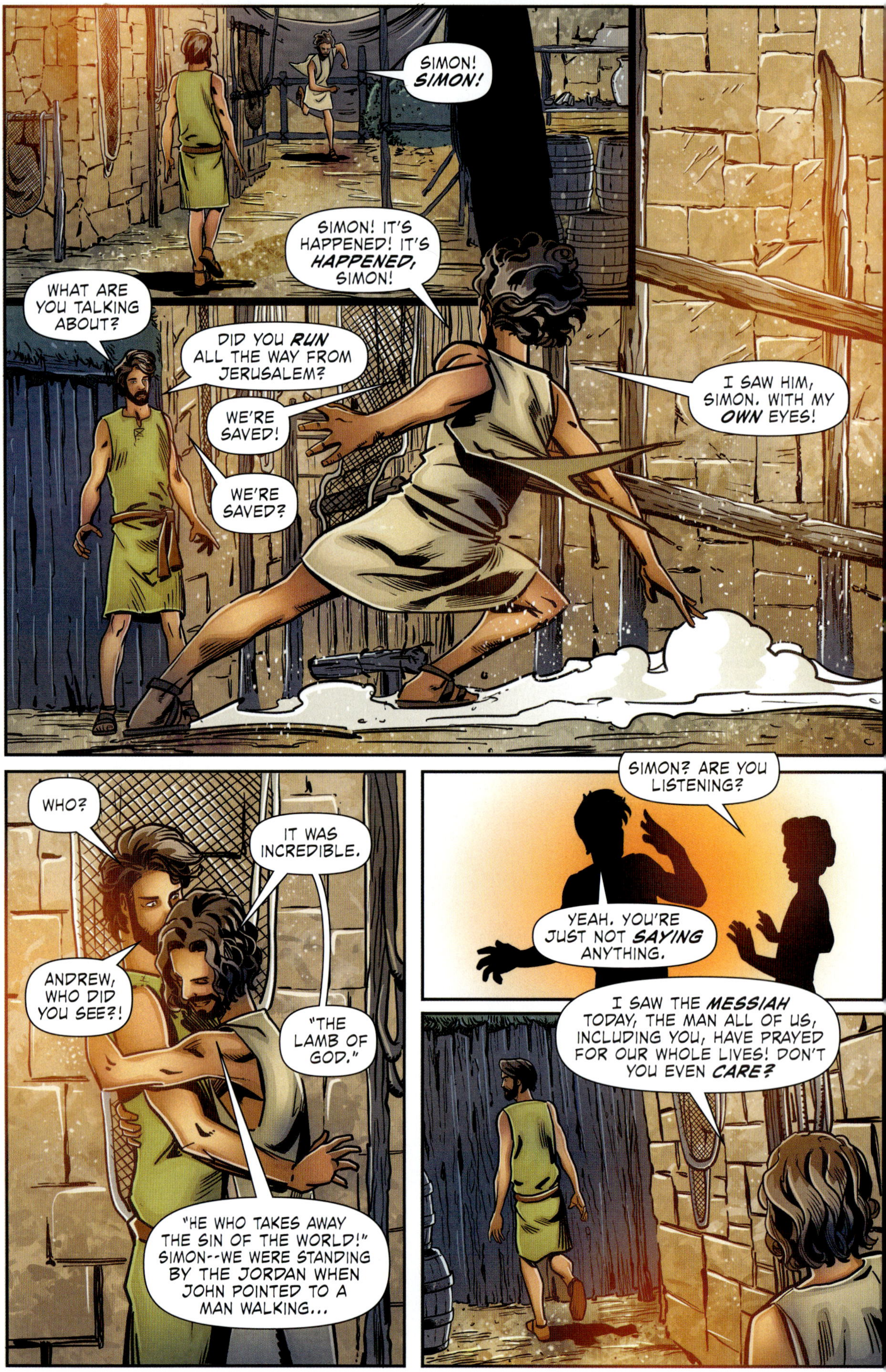

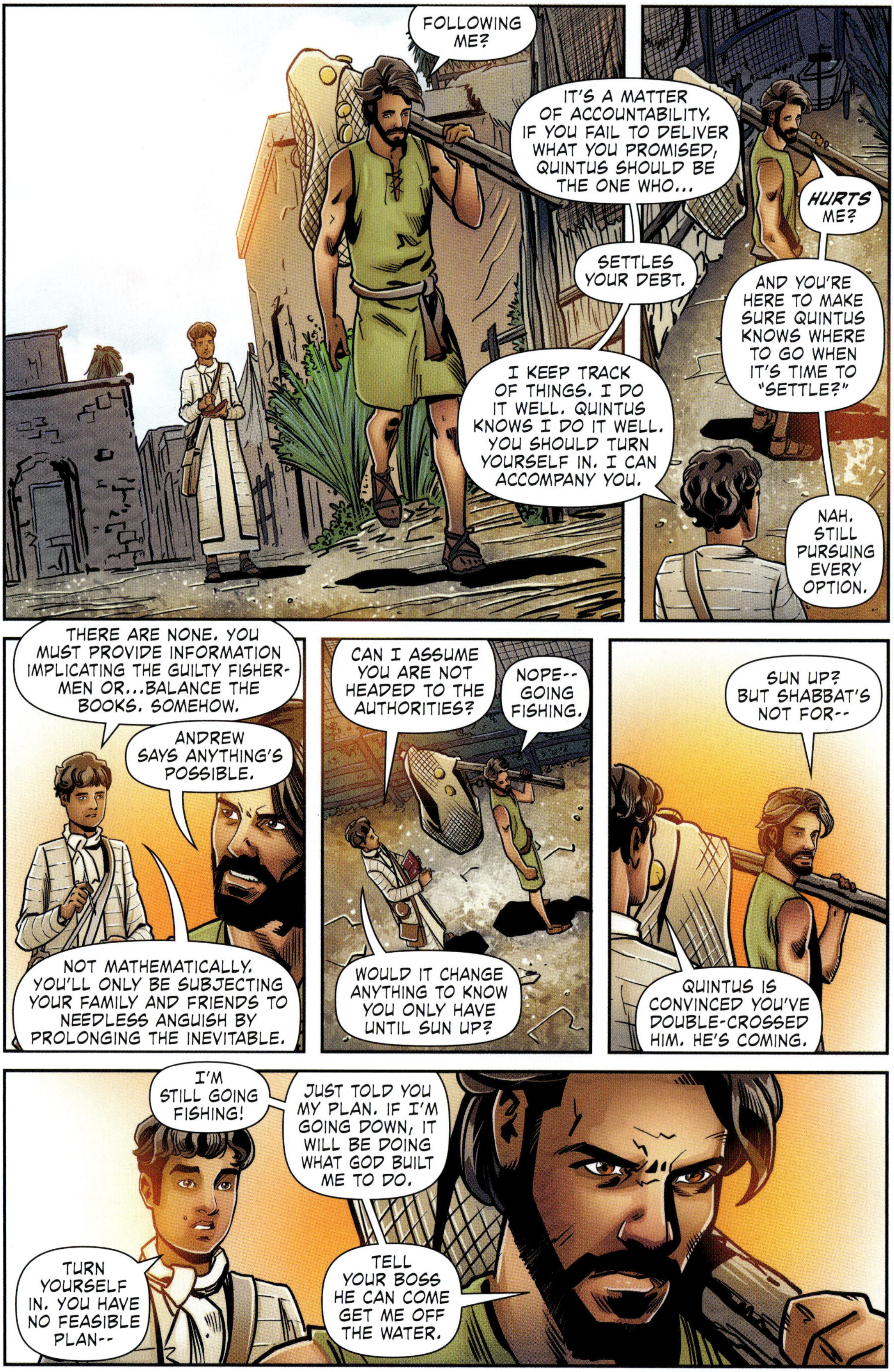

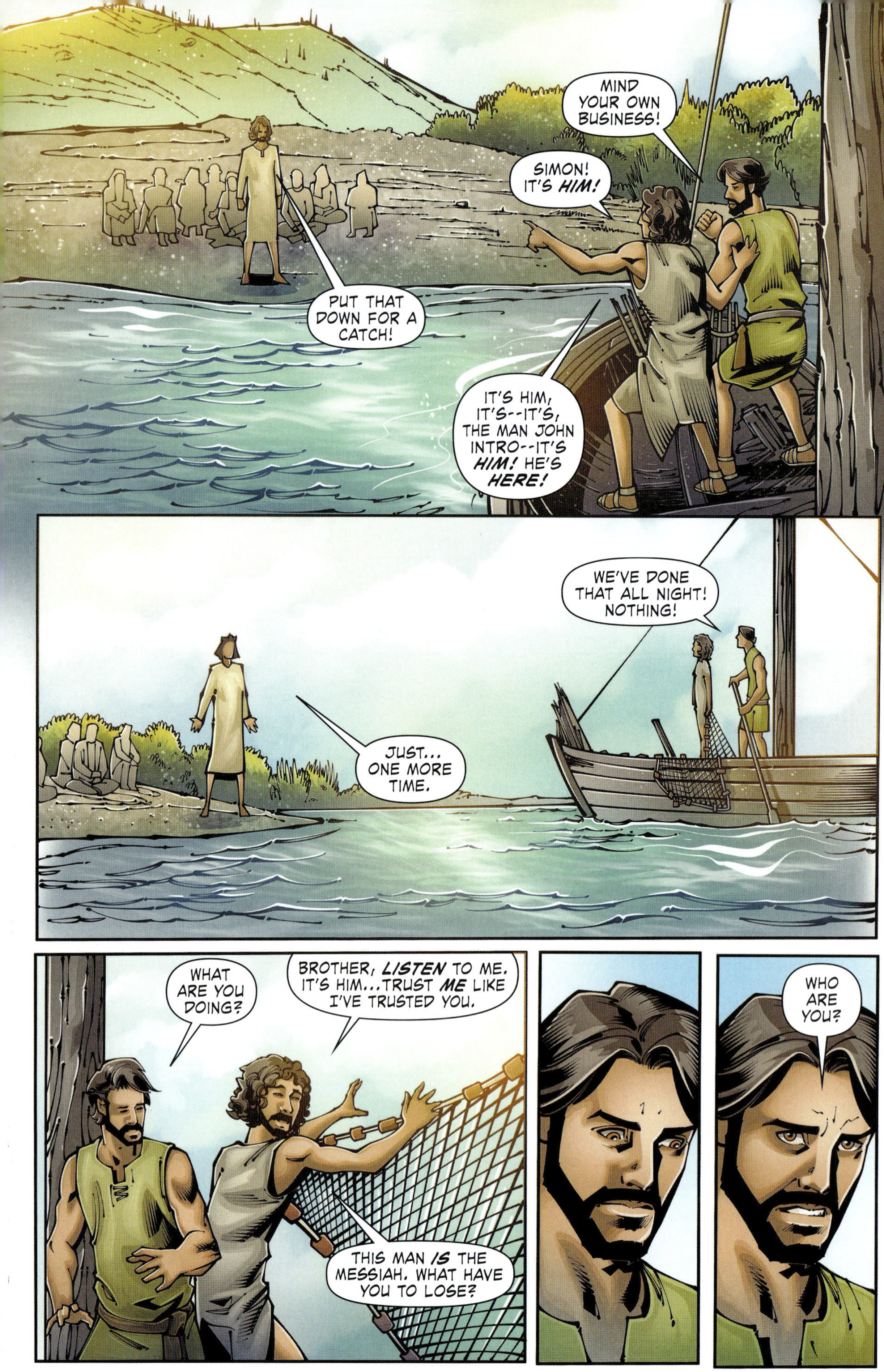

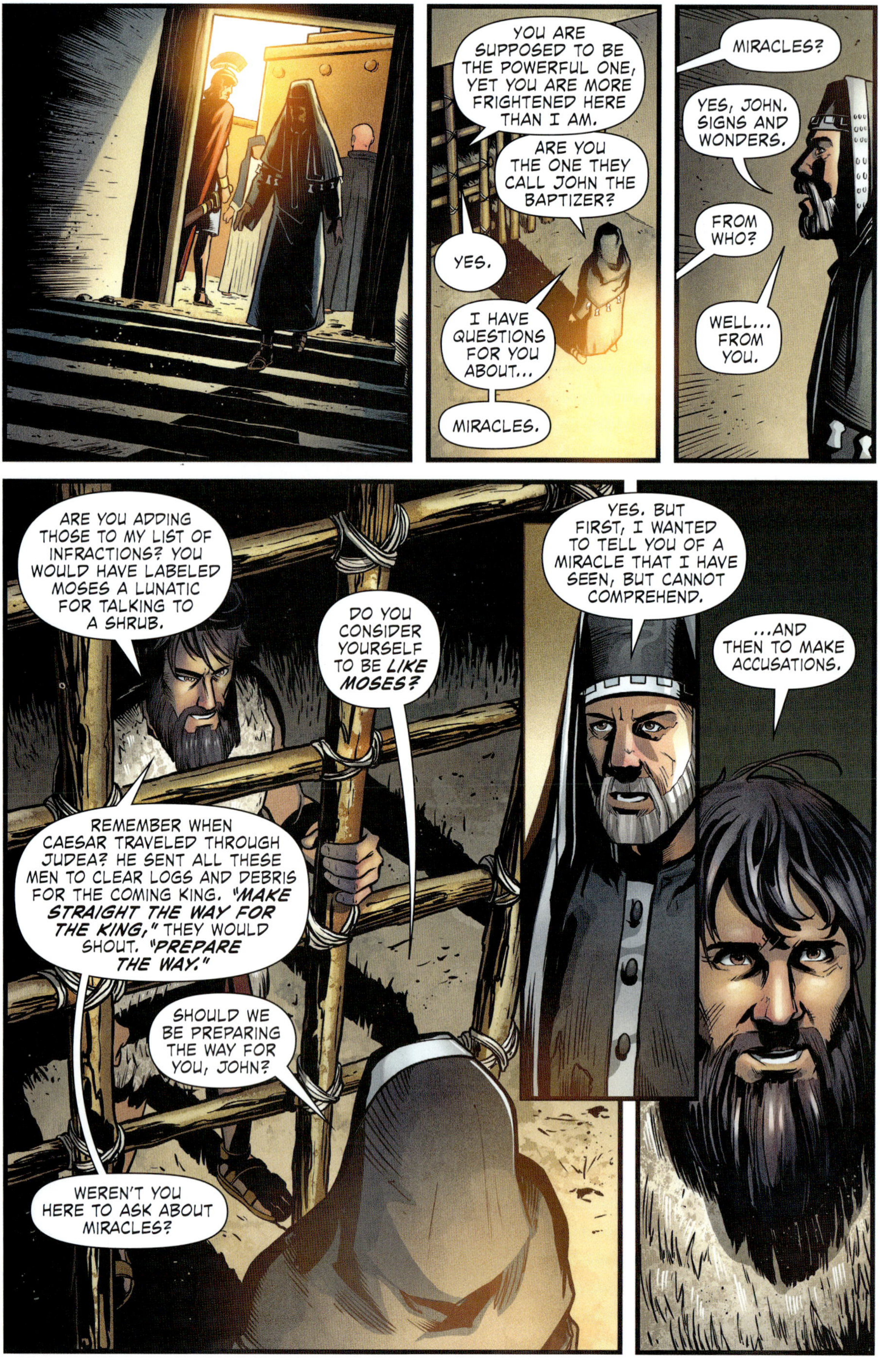

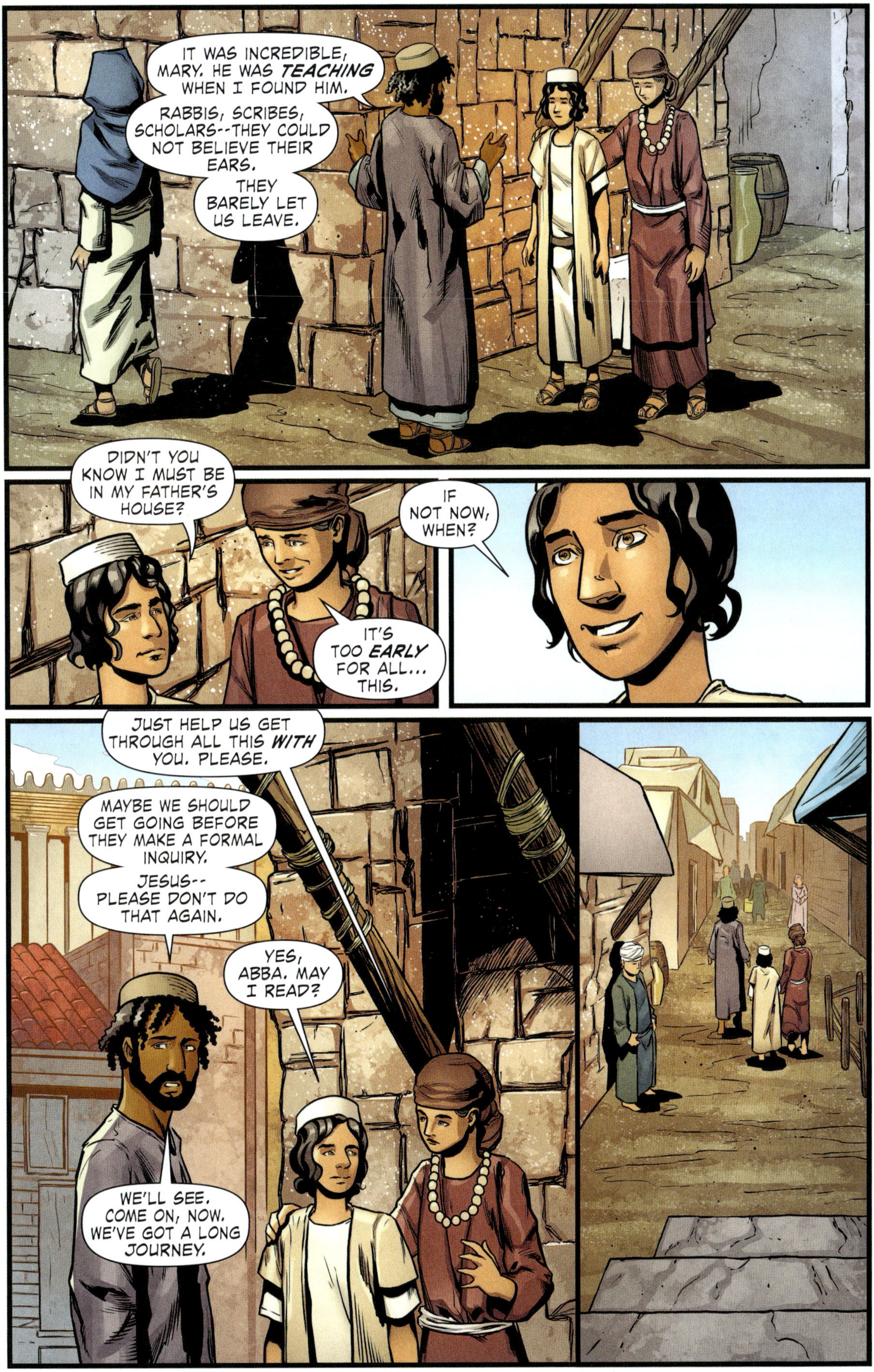

It was incredible, Mary. He was *teaching* when I found him.

Rabbis, scribes, scholars--they could not believe their ears.

They barely let us leave.

Didn't you know I must be in my father's house?

It's too *early* for all... this.

If not now, when?

Just help us get through all this *with* you. Please.

Maybe we should get going before they make a formal inquiry.

Jesus-- please don't do that again.

Yes, Abba. May I read?

We'll see. Come on, now. We've got a long journey.

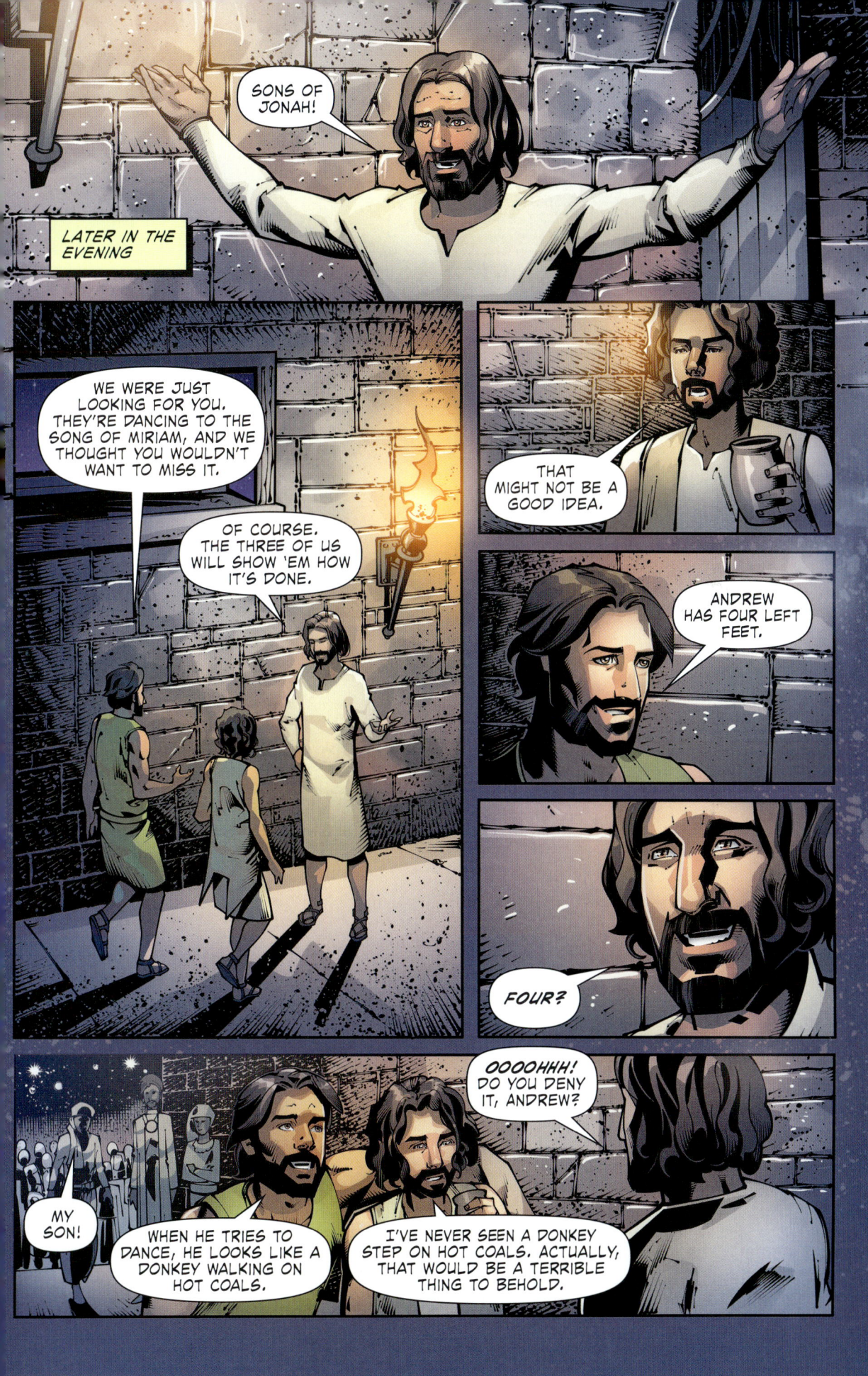

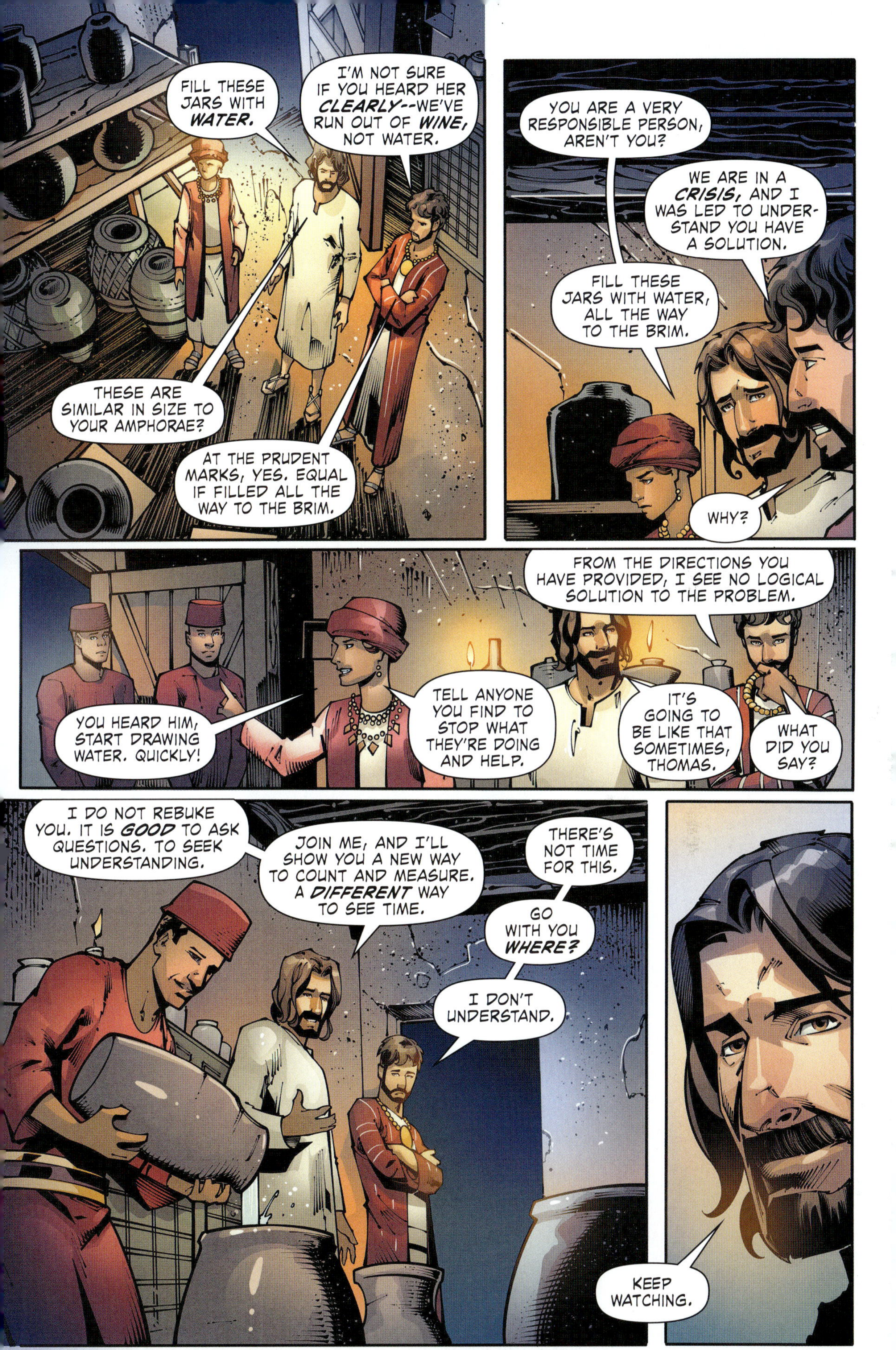

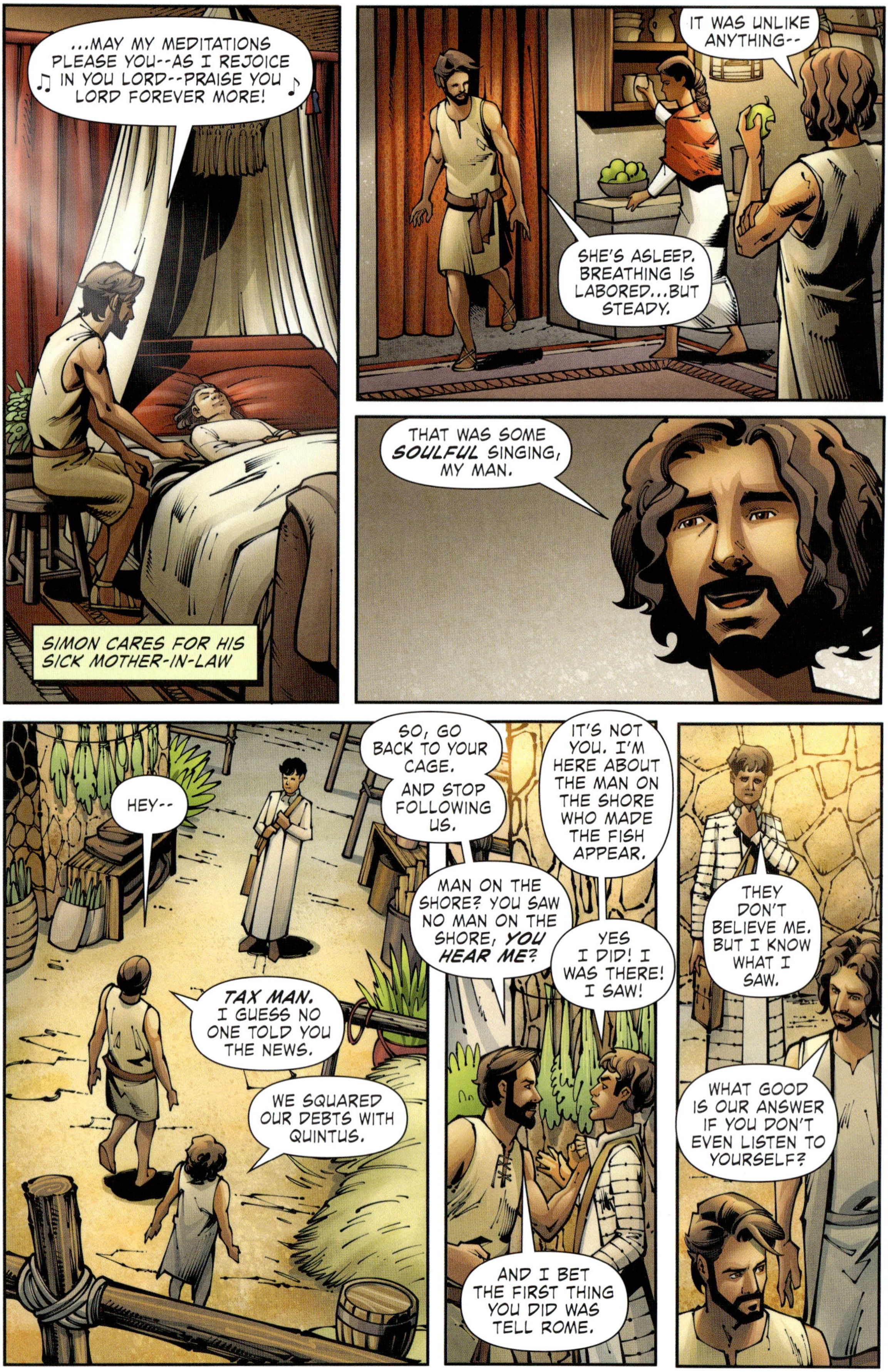

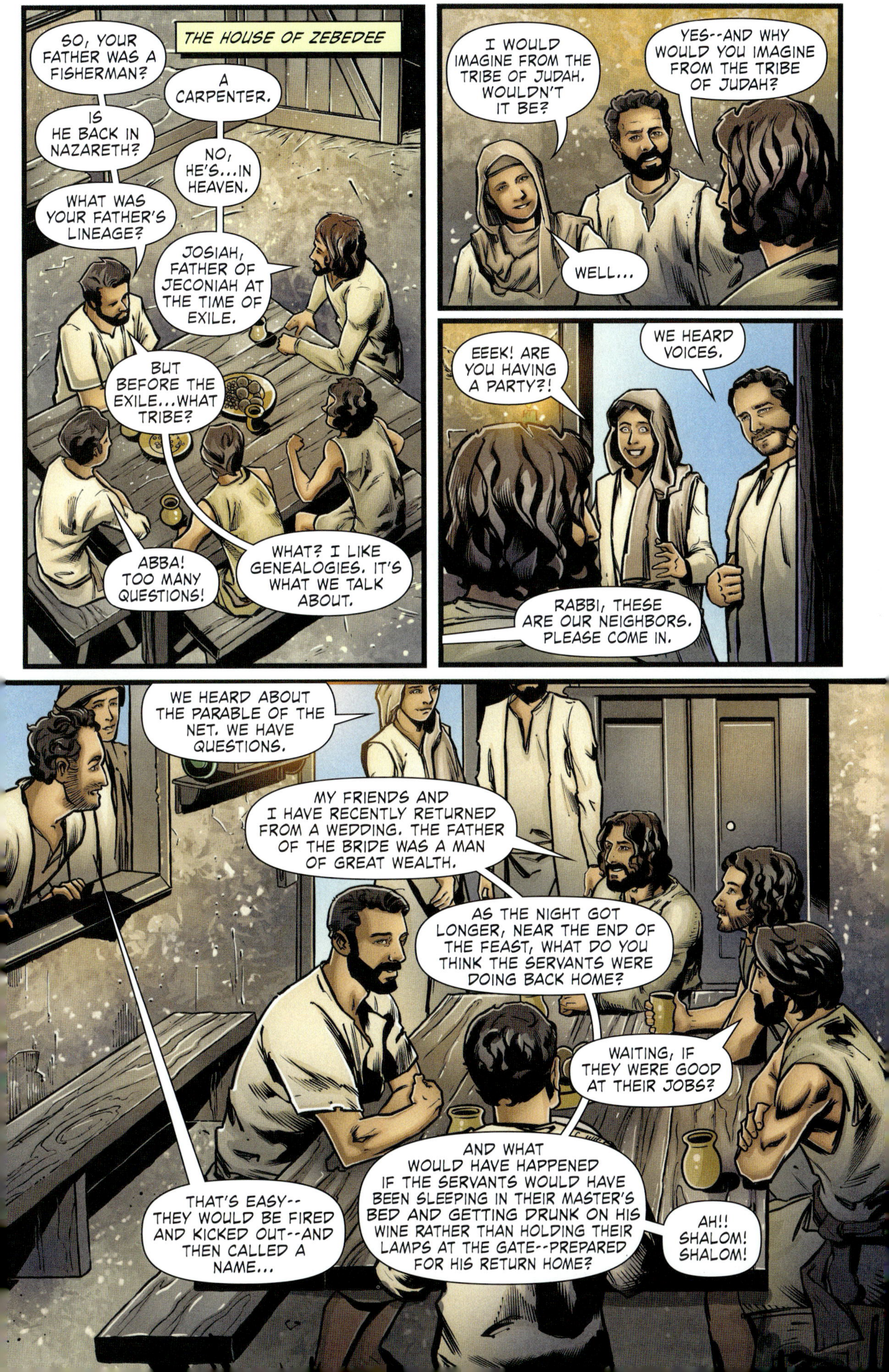

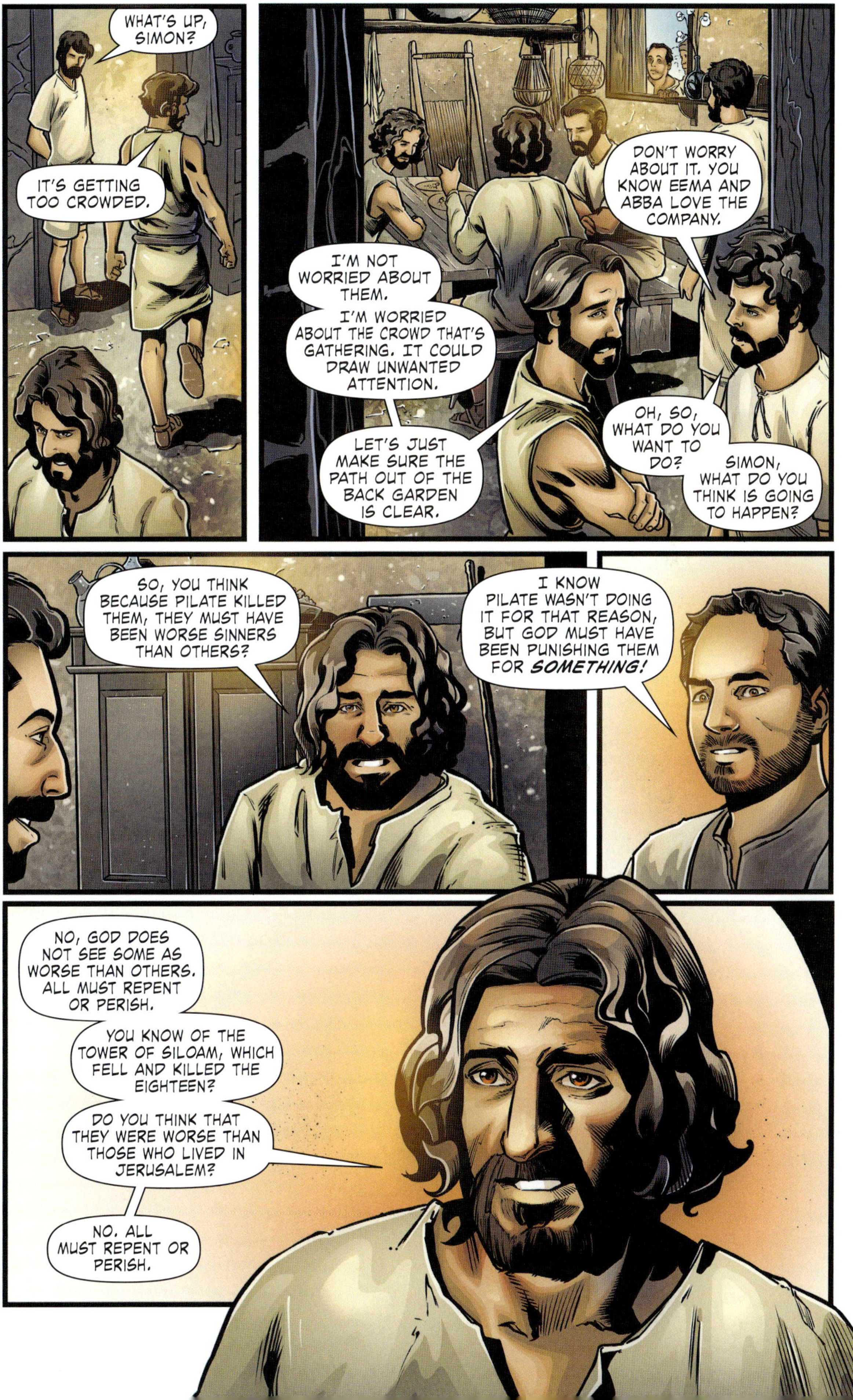

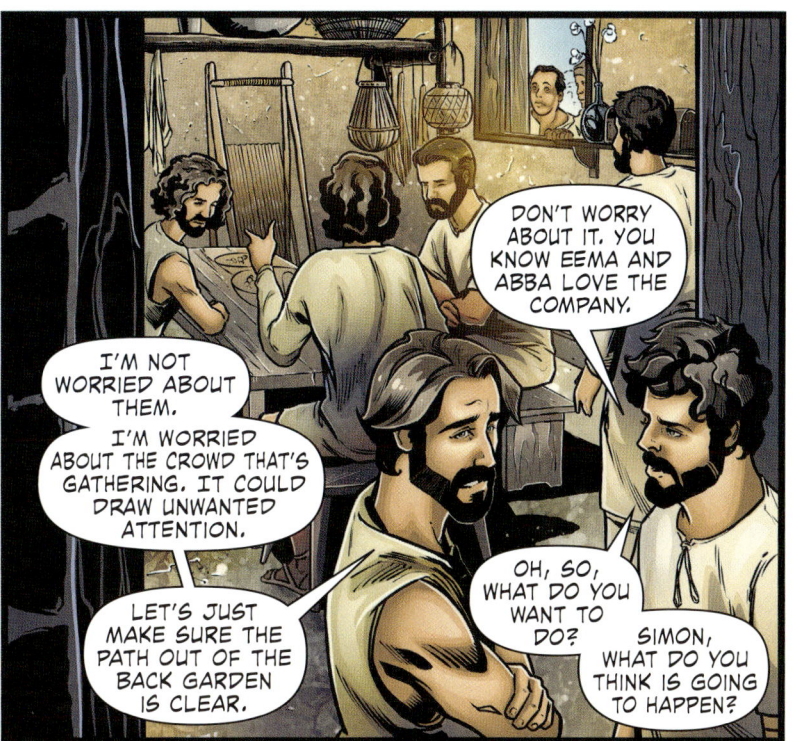

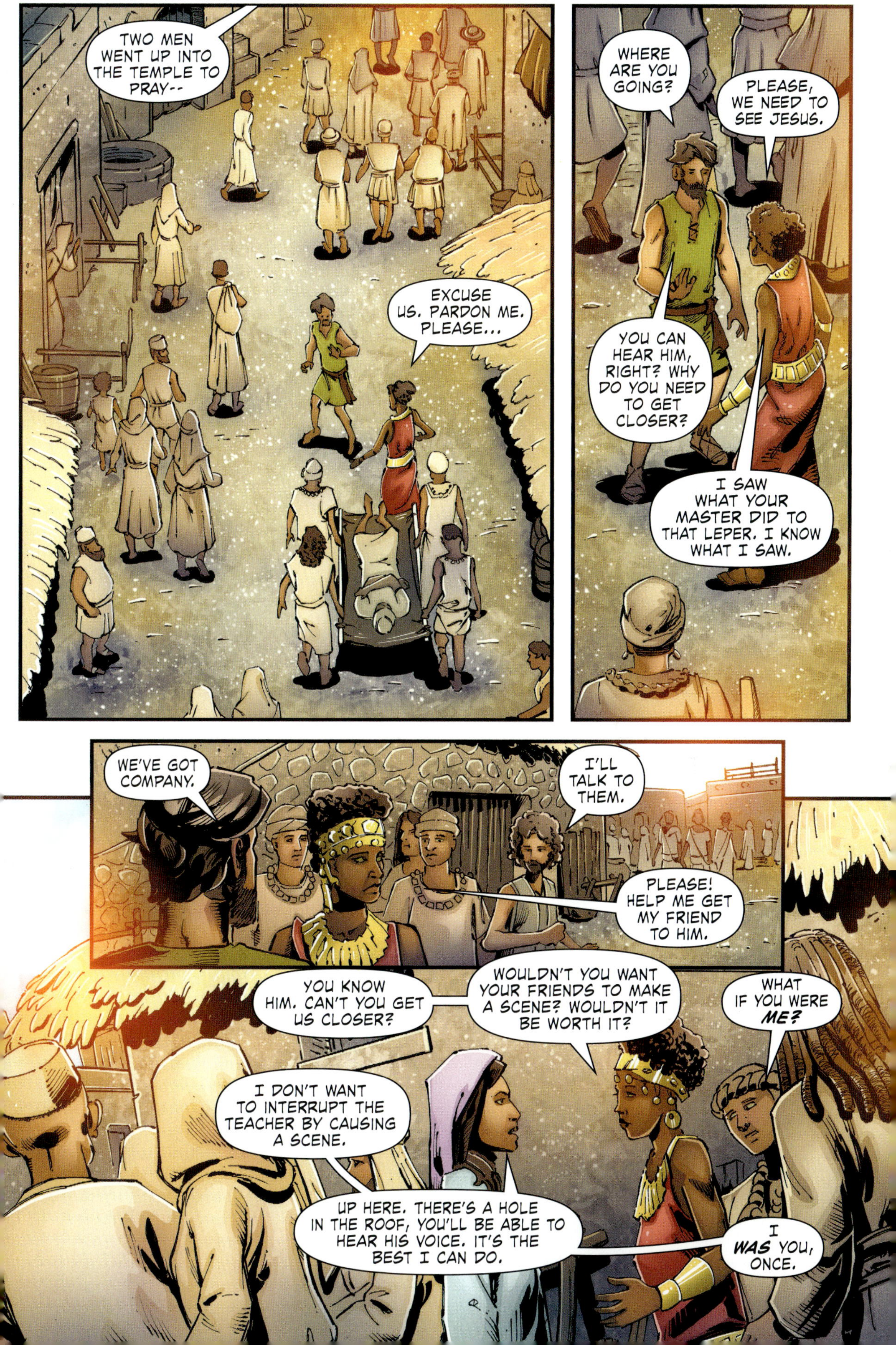

IT'S OKAY! COME UP!

HOW DID YOU GET UP THERE?

WE CLIMBED THE LADDER. IT'S EASY.

WELL, THE MAN SPEAKING IS CALLED--

--JESUS OF NAZARETH.

WE KNOW HIM.

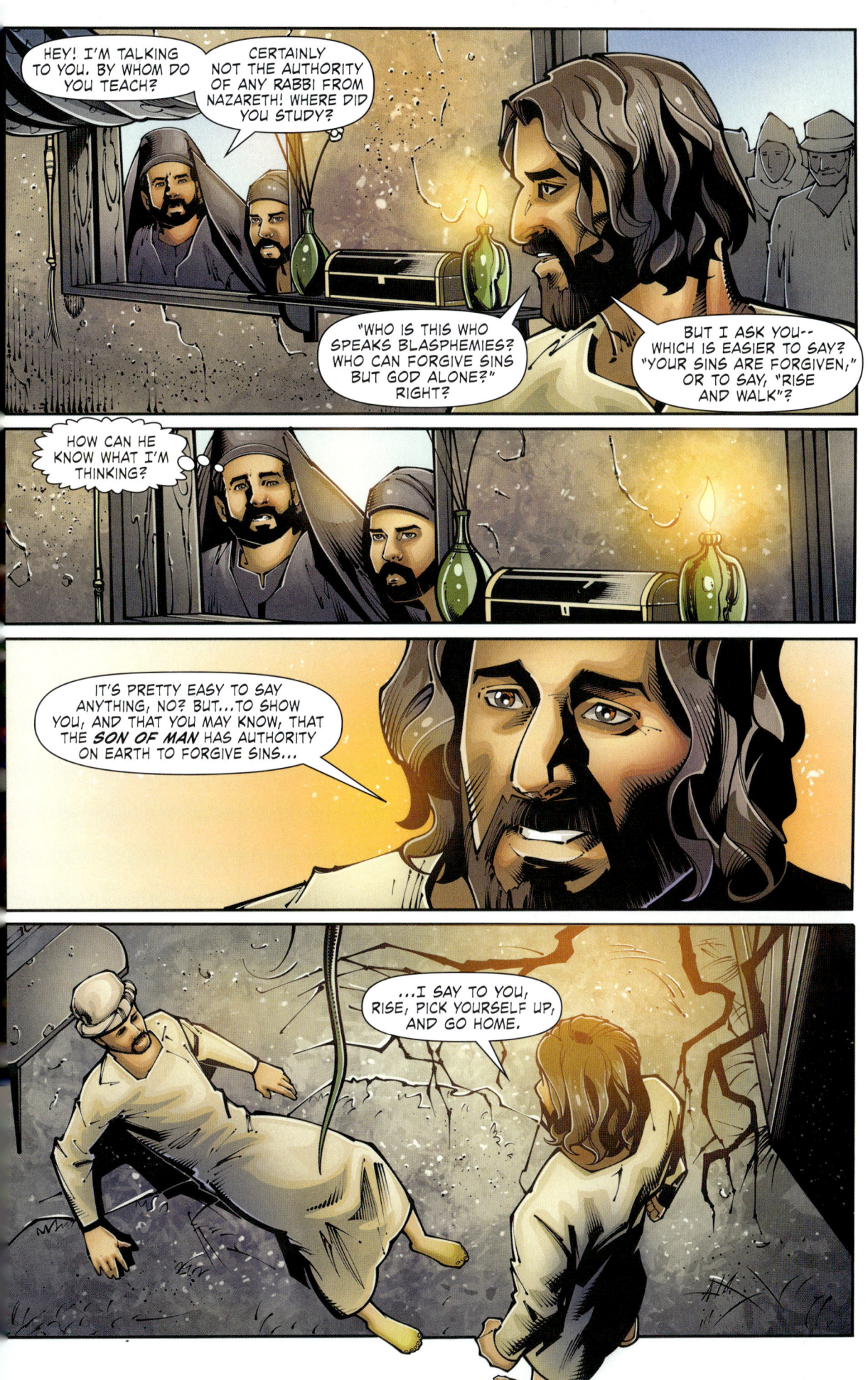

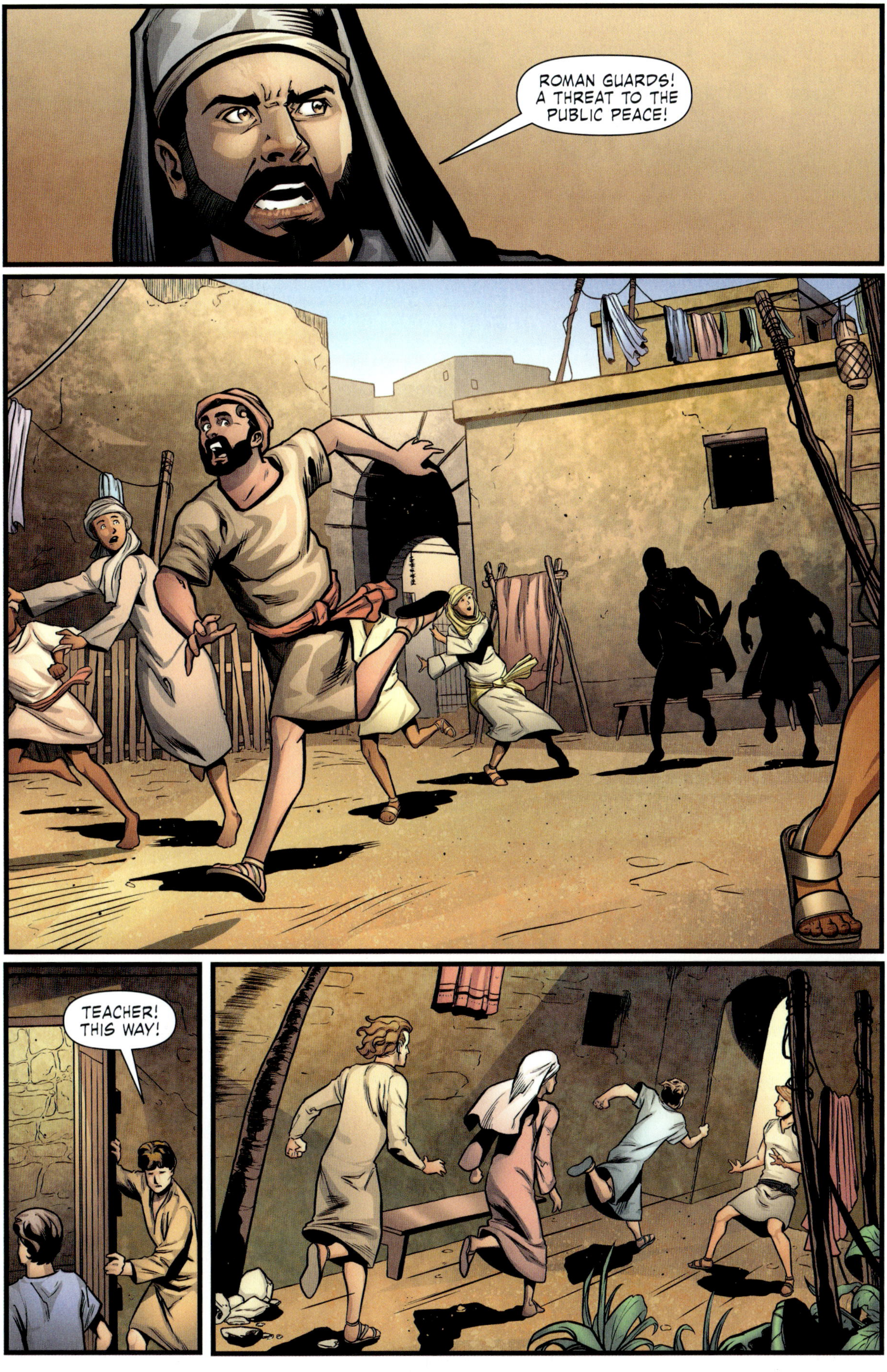

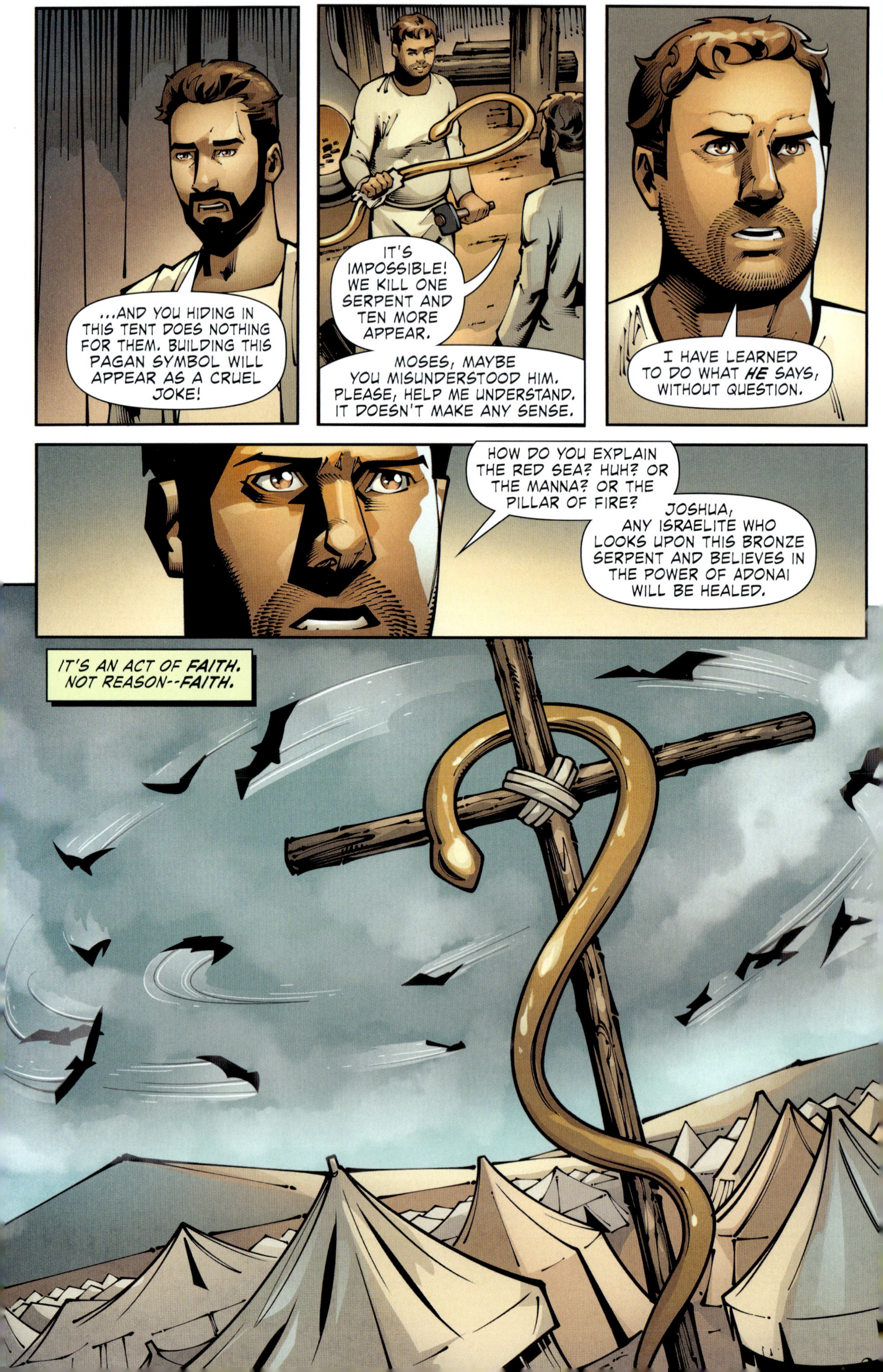

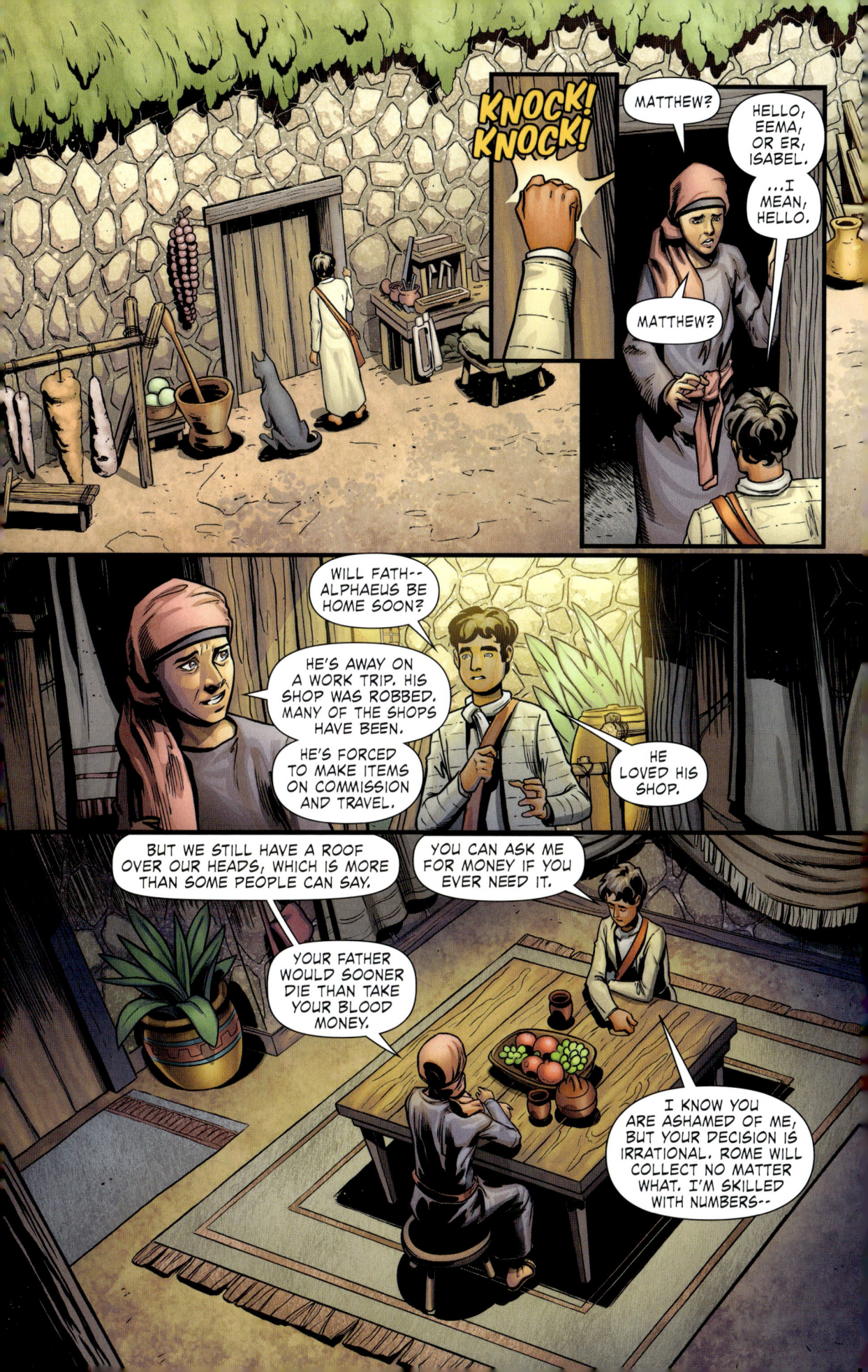

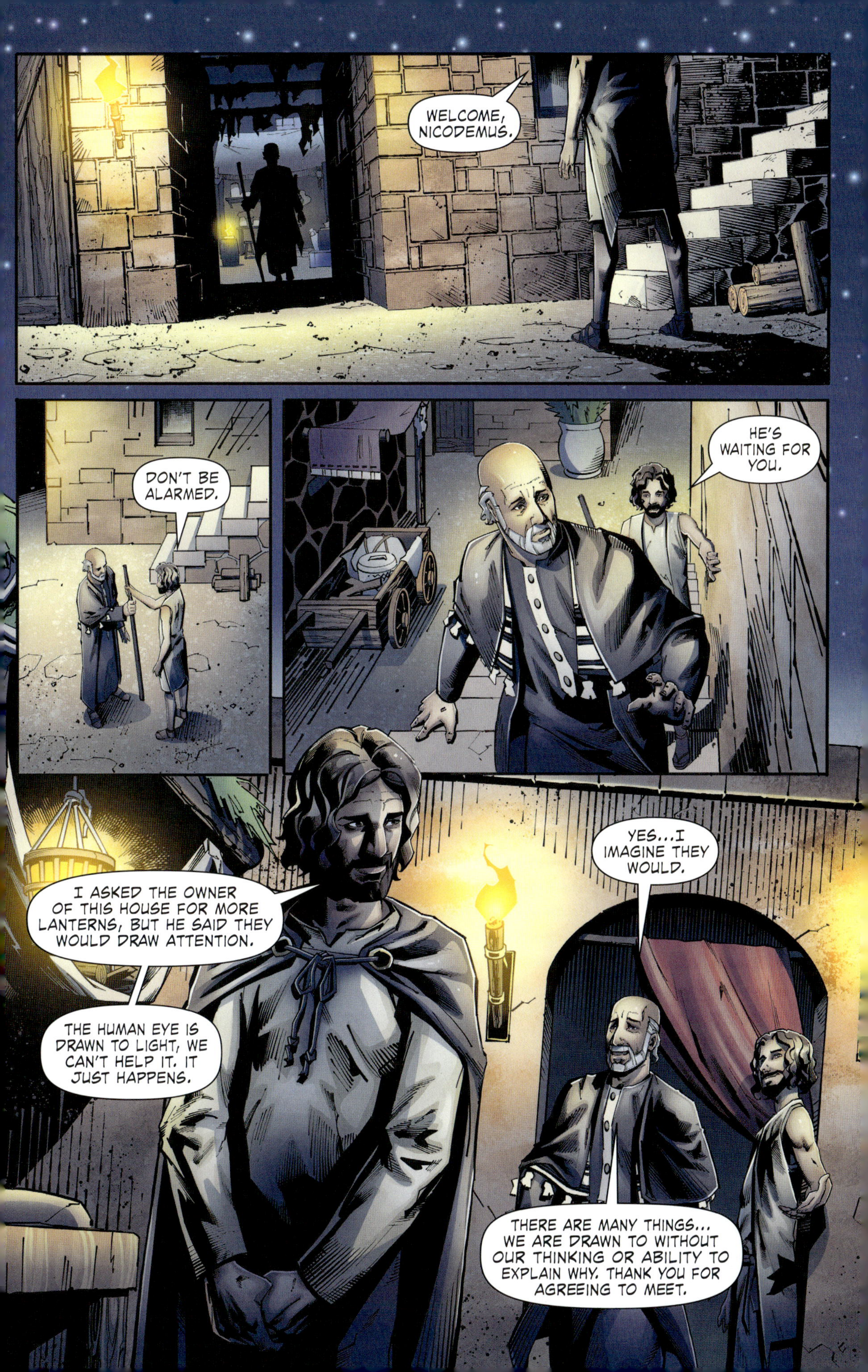

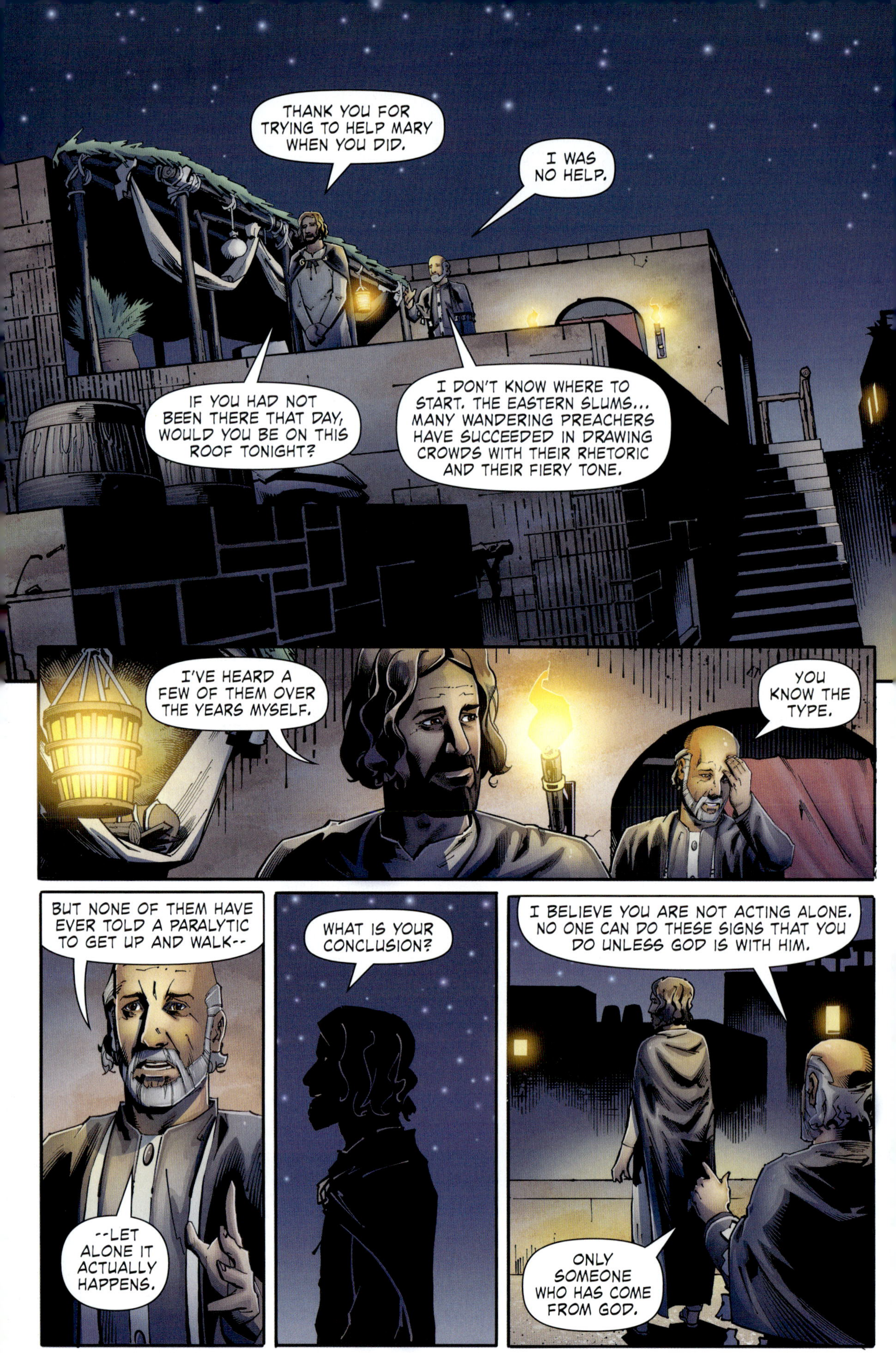

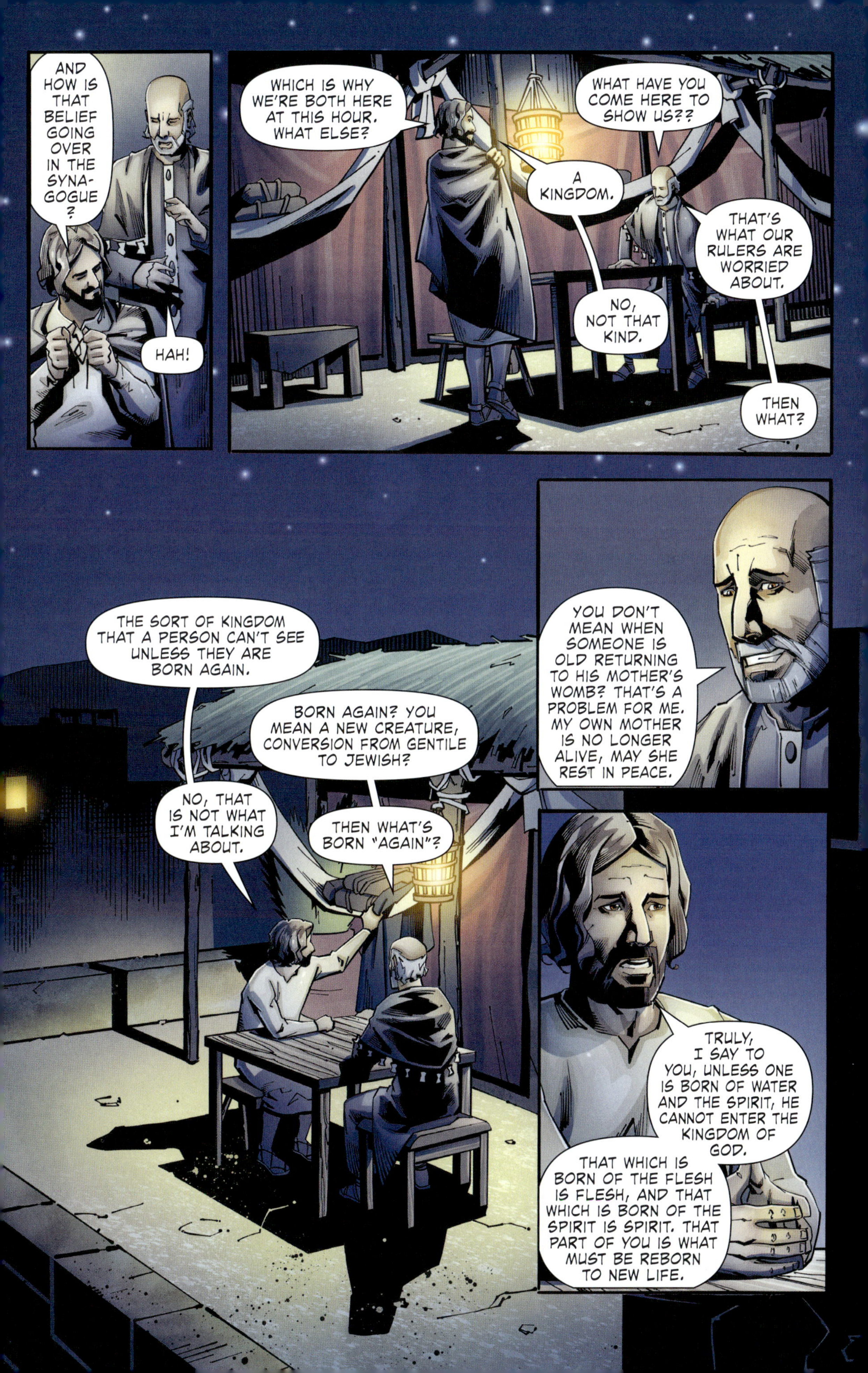

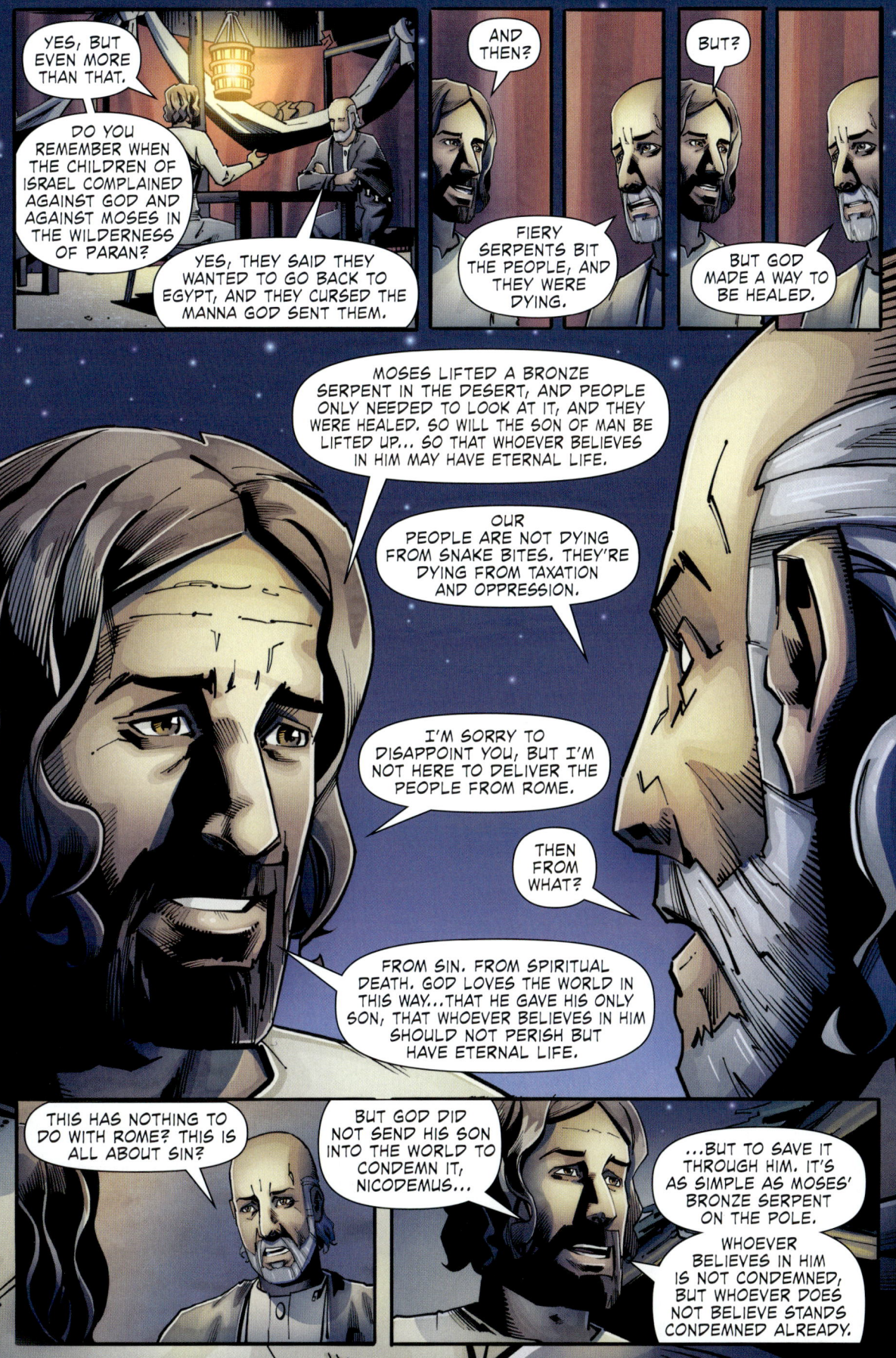

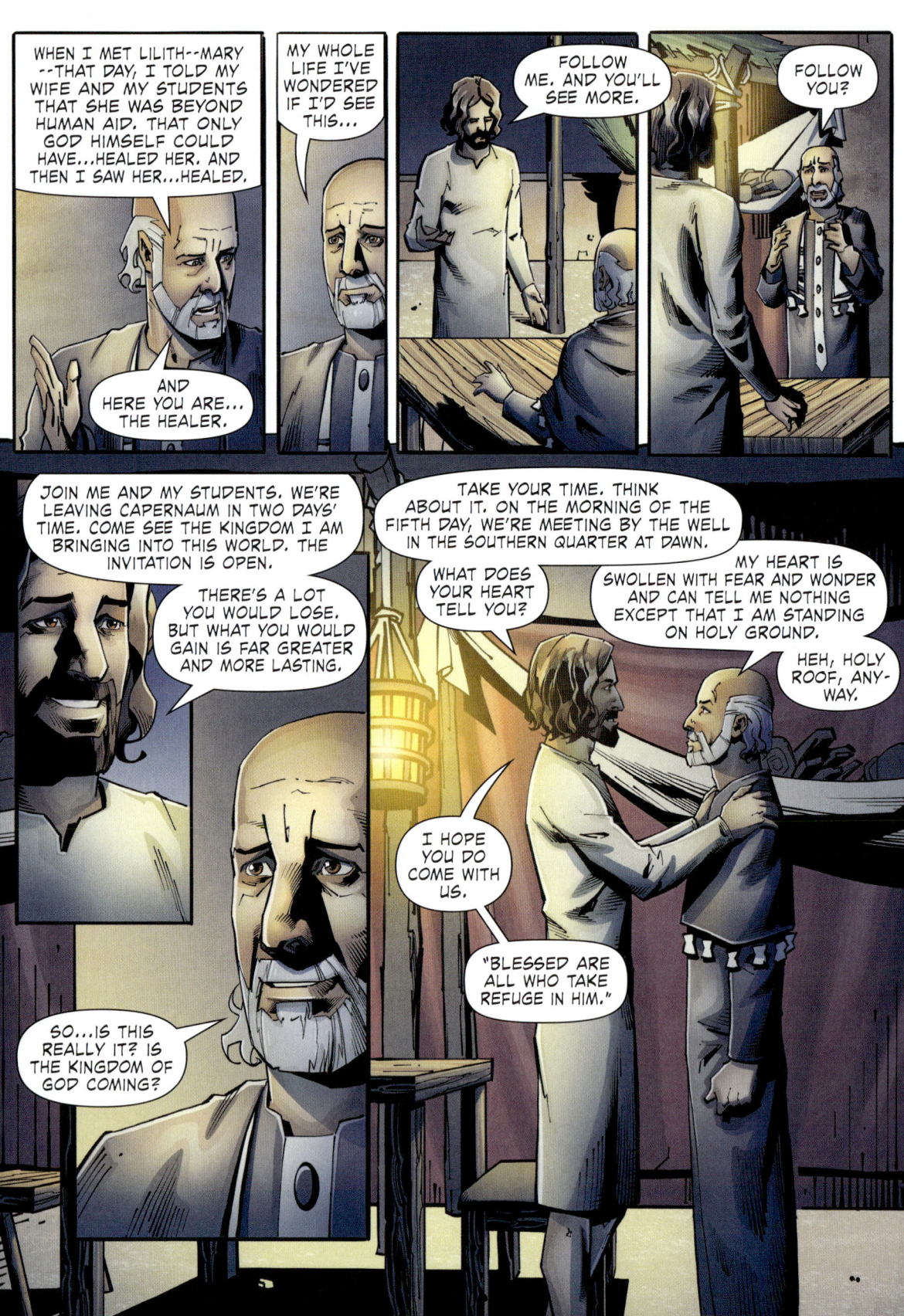

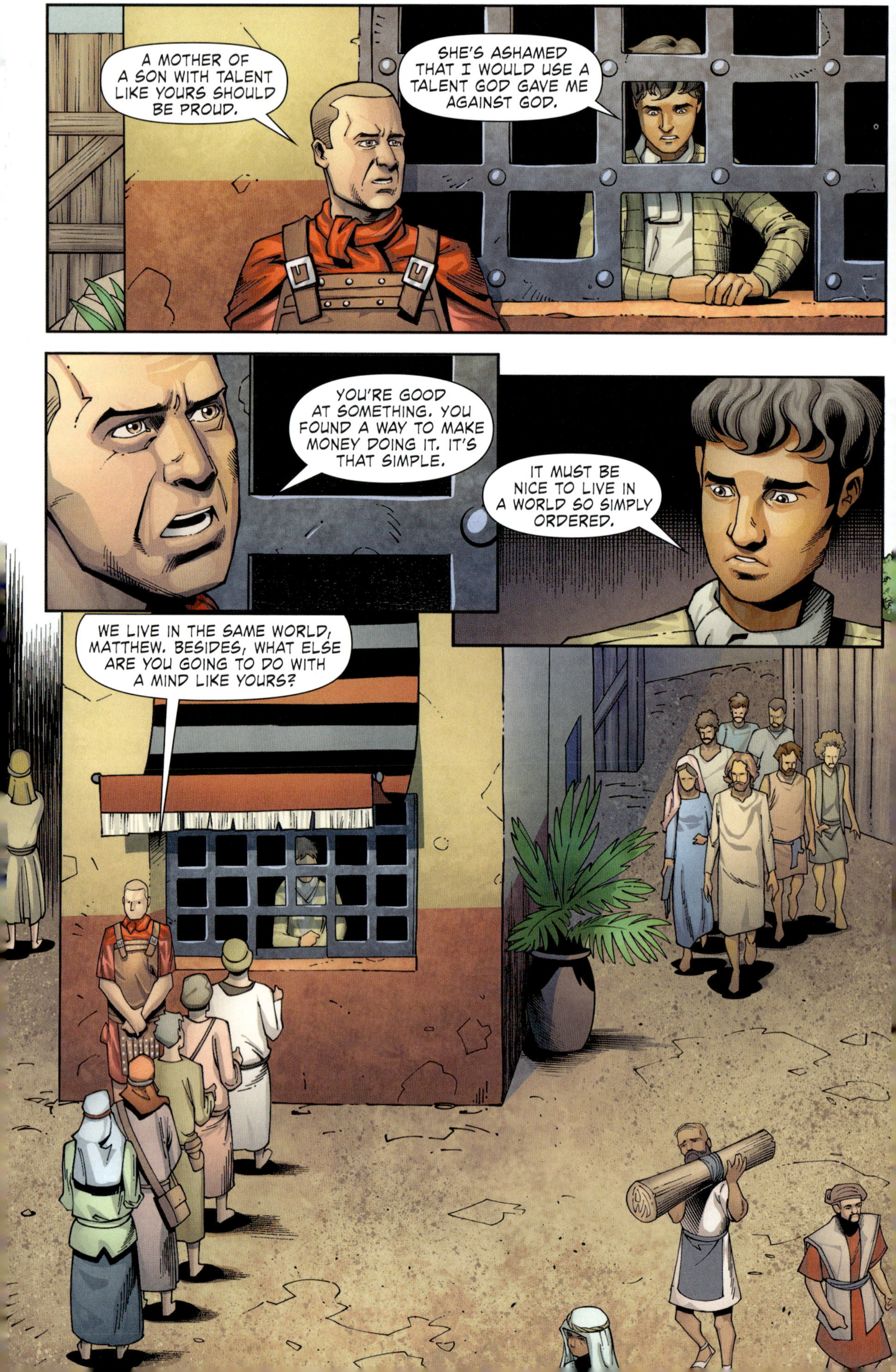

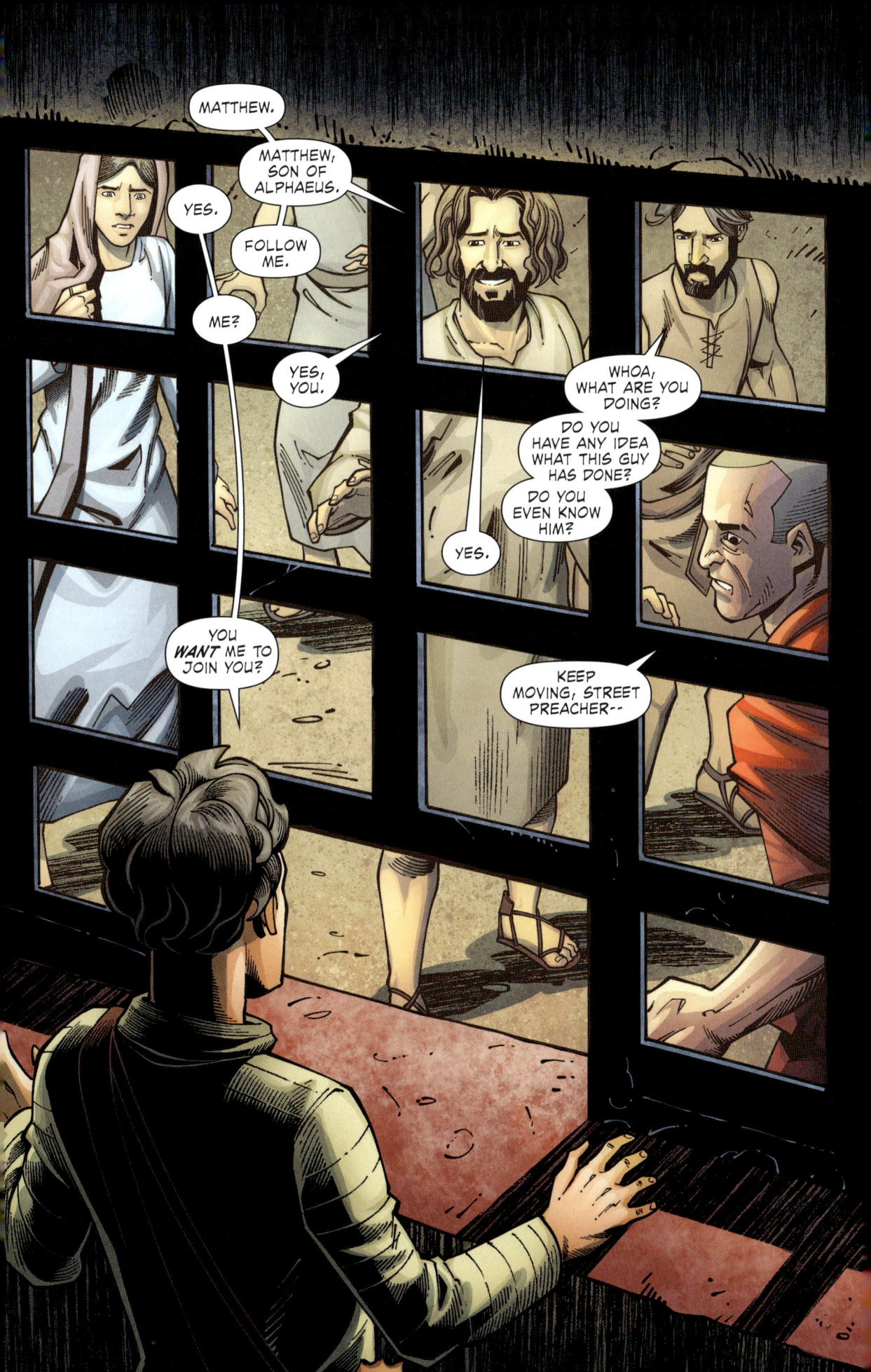

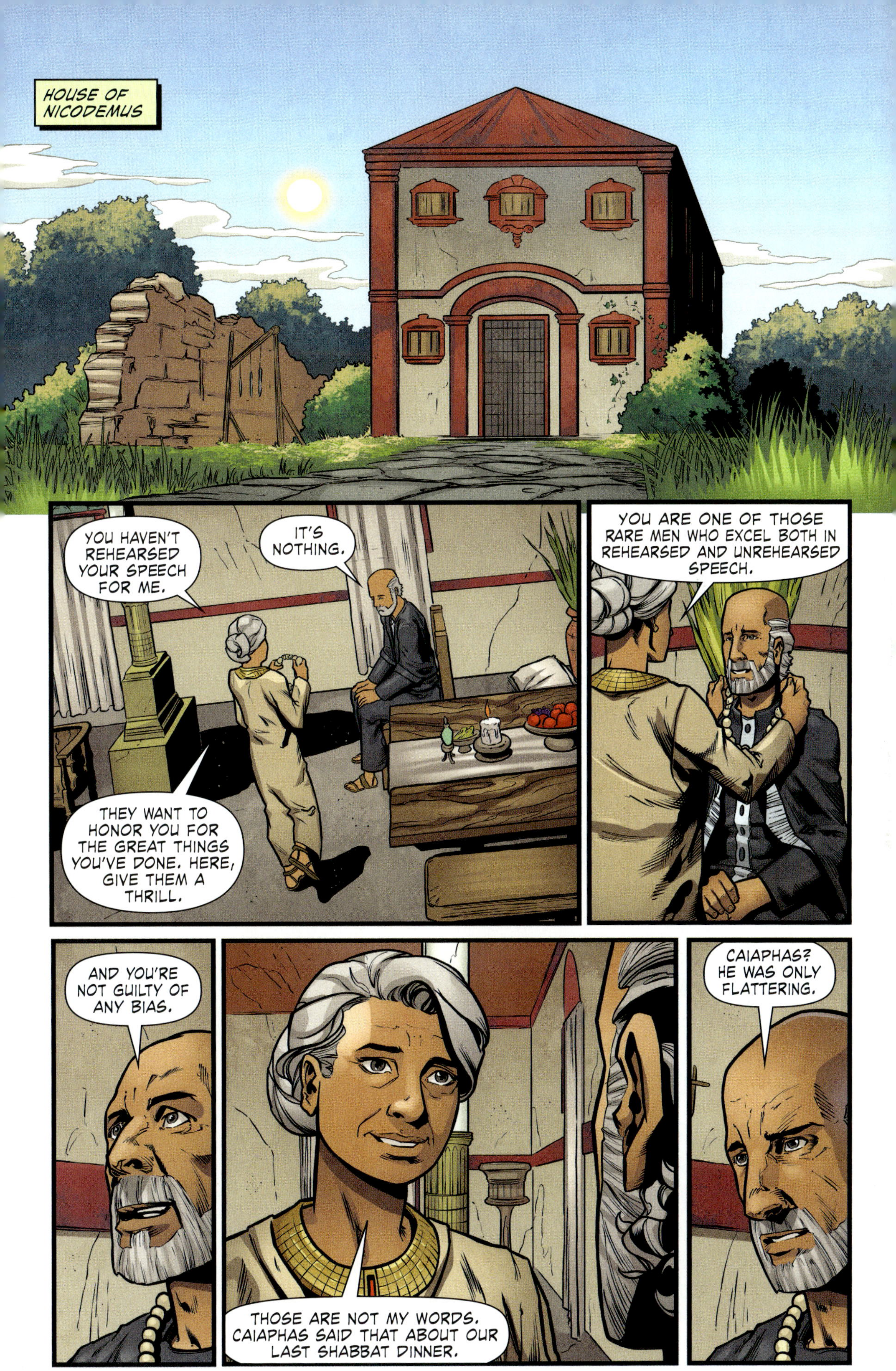

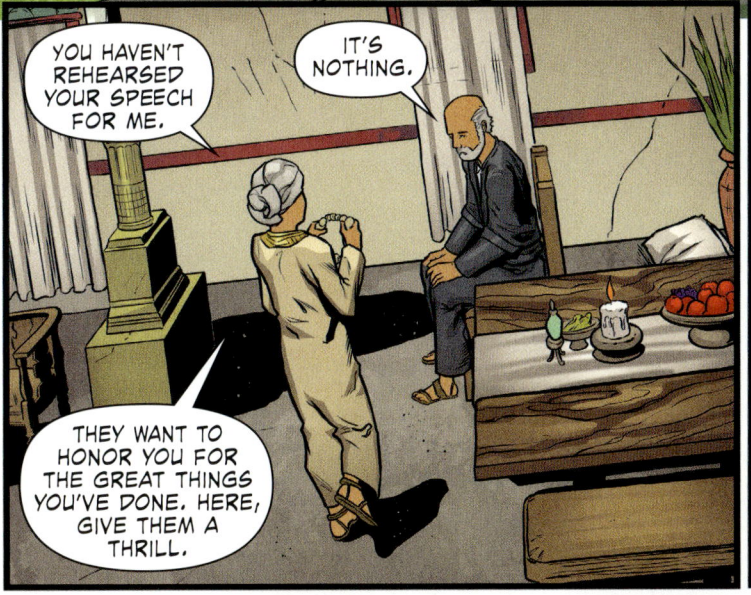

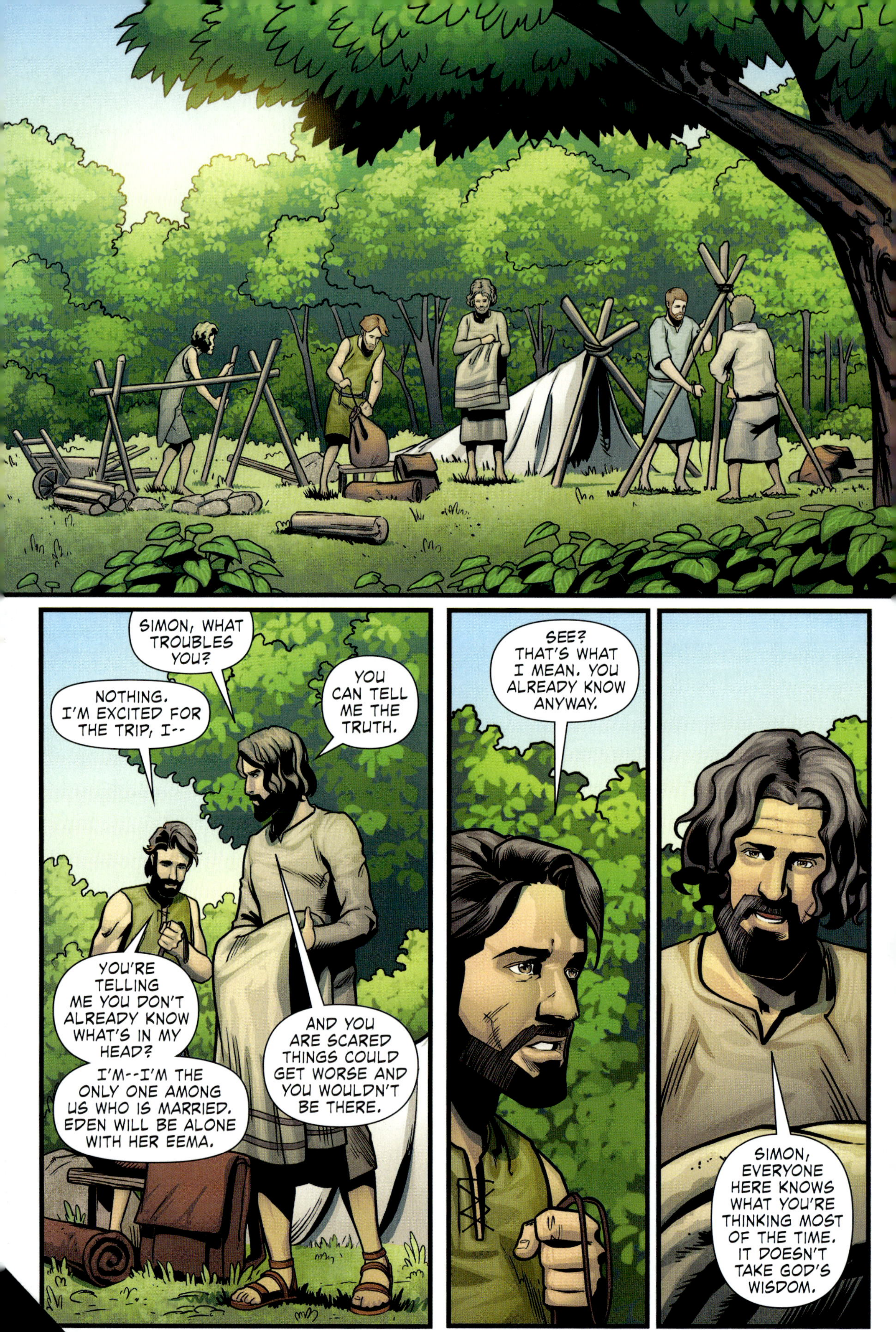

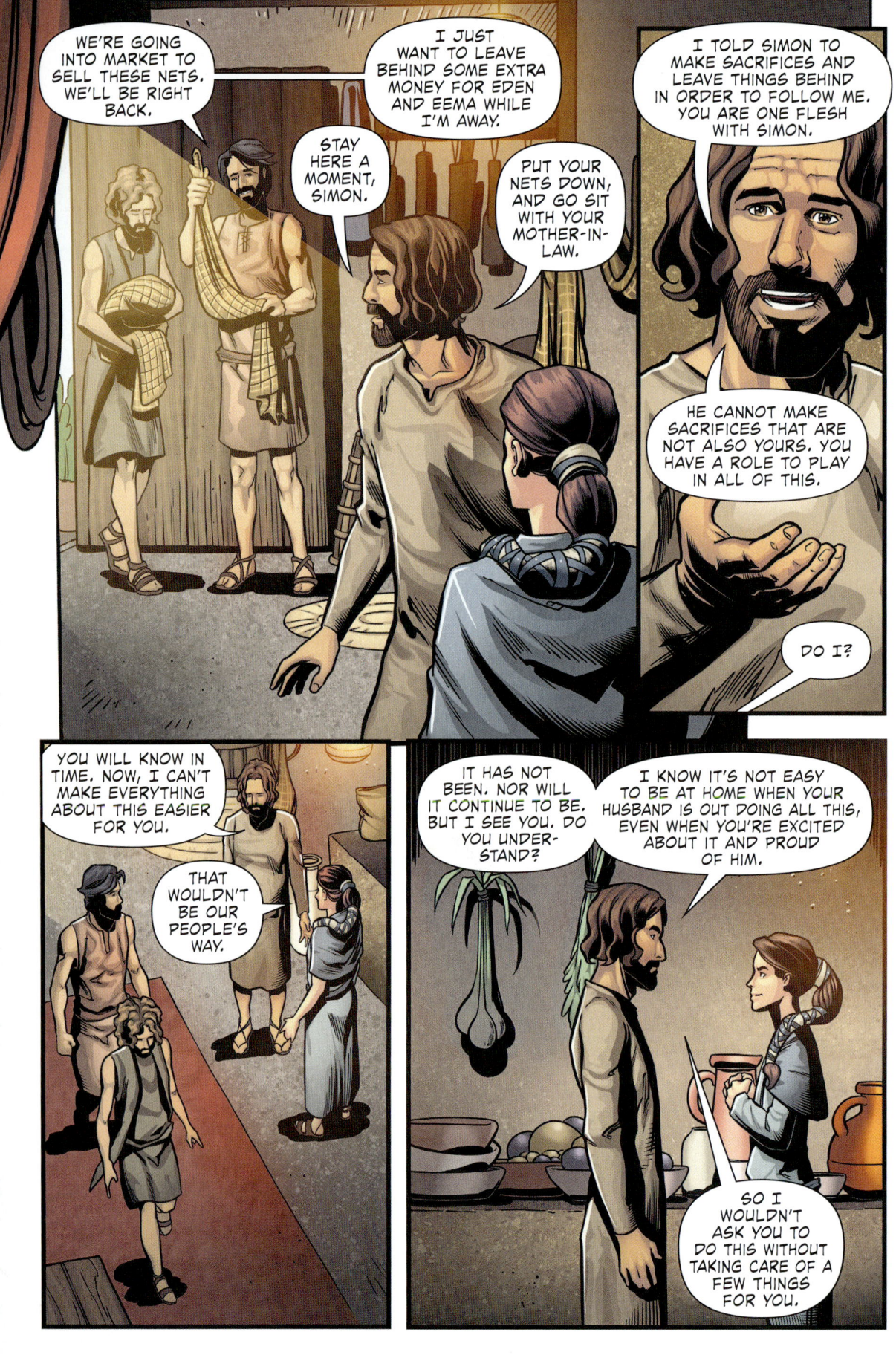

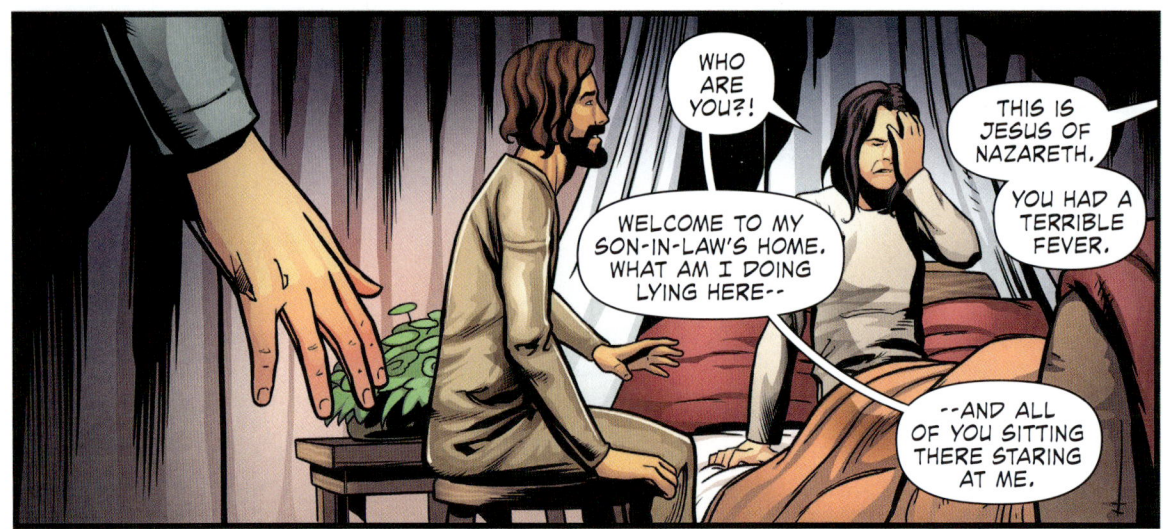

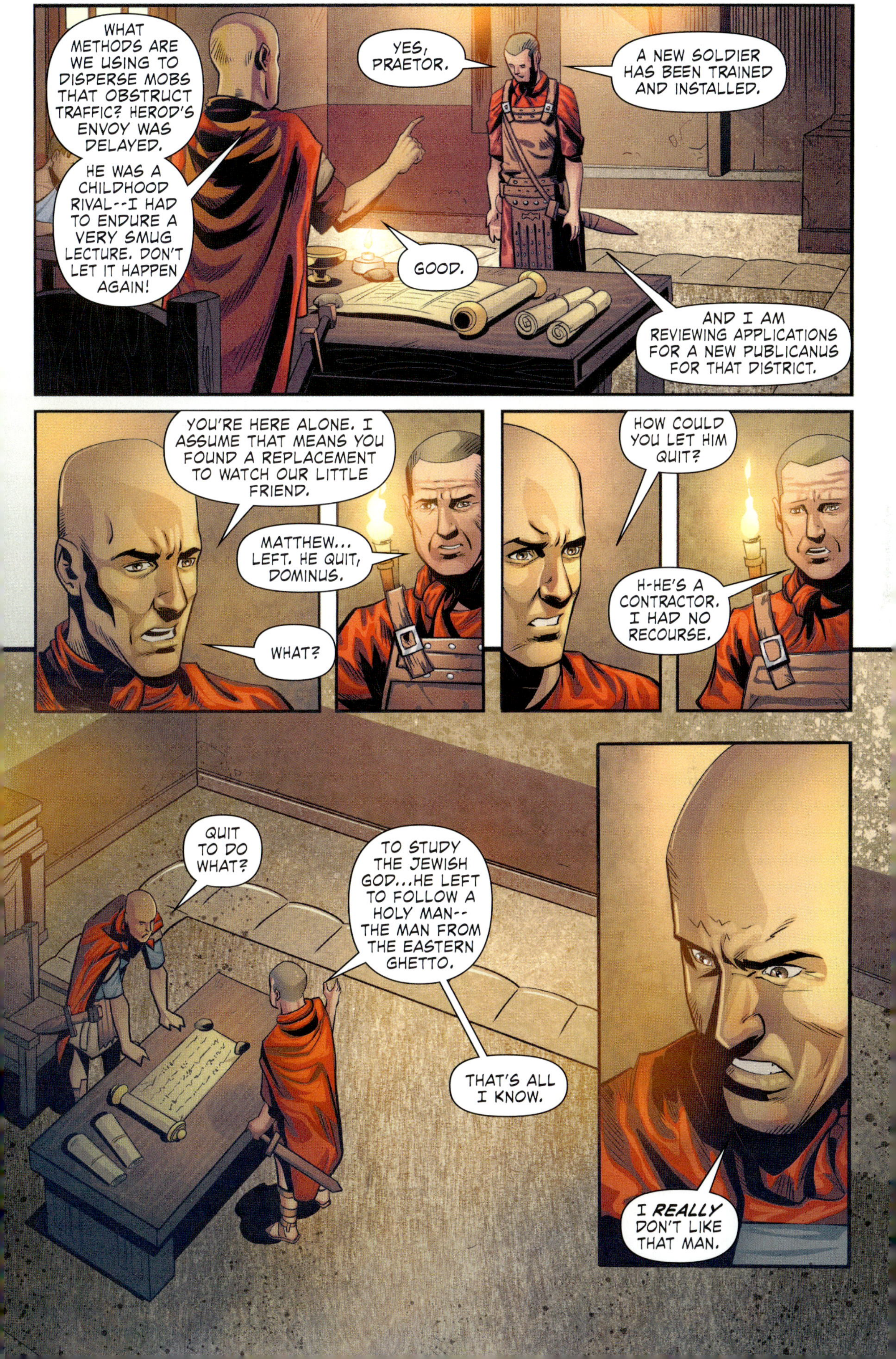

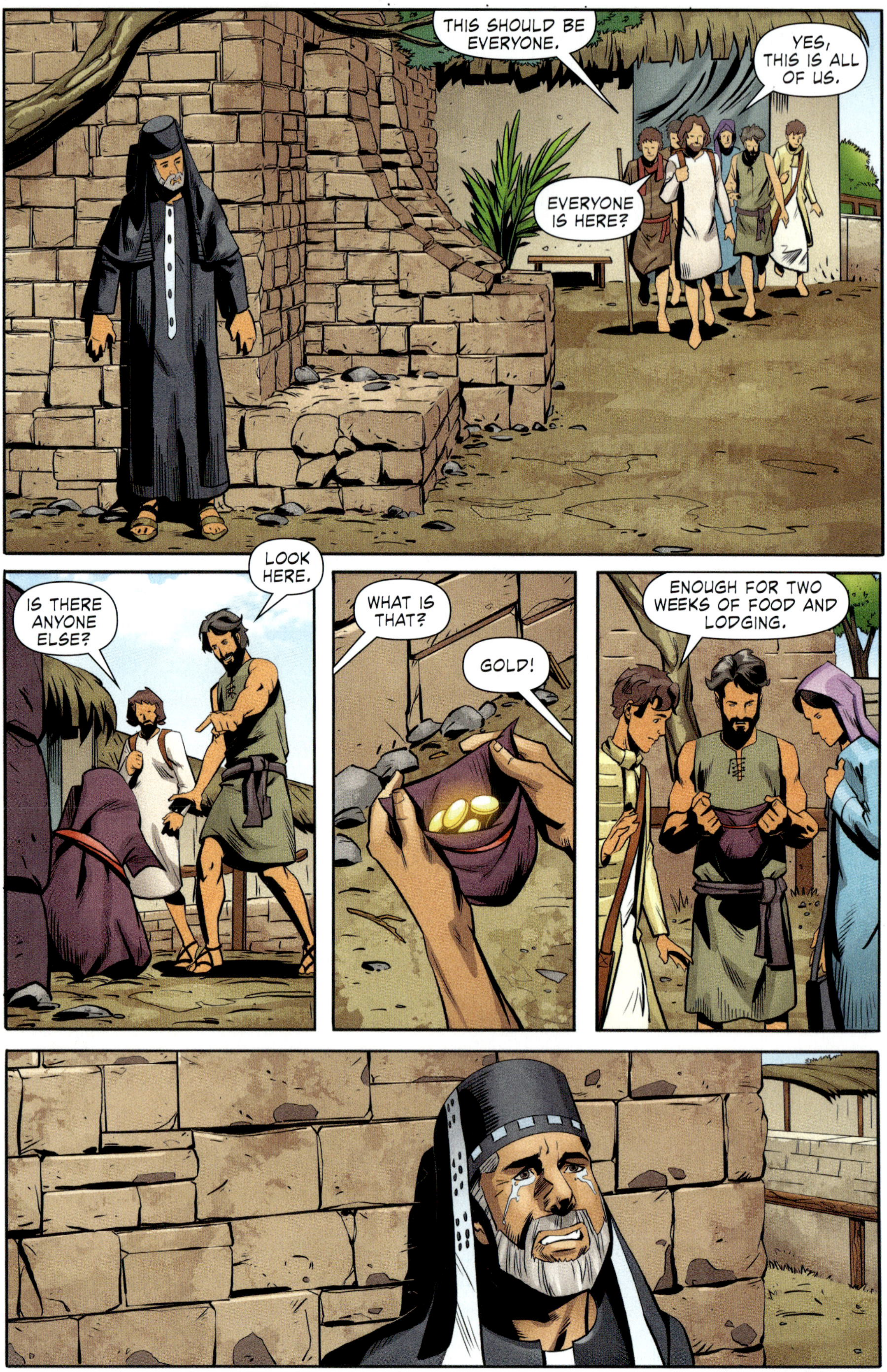

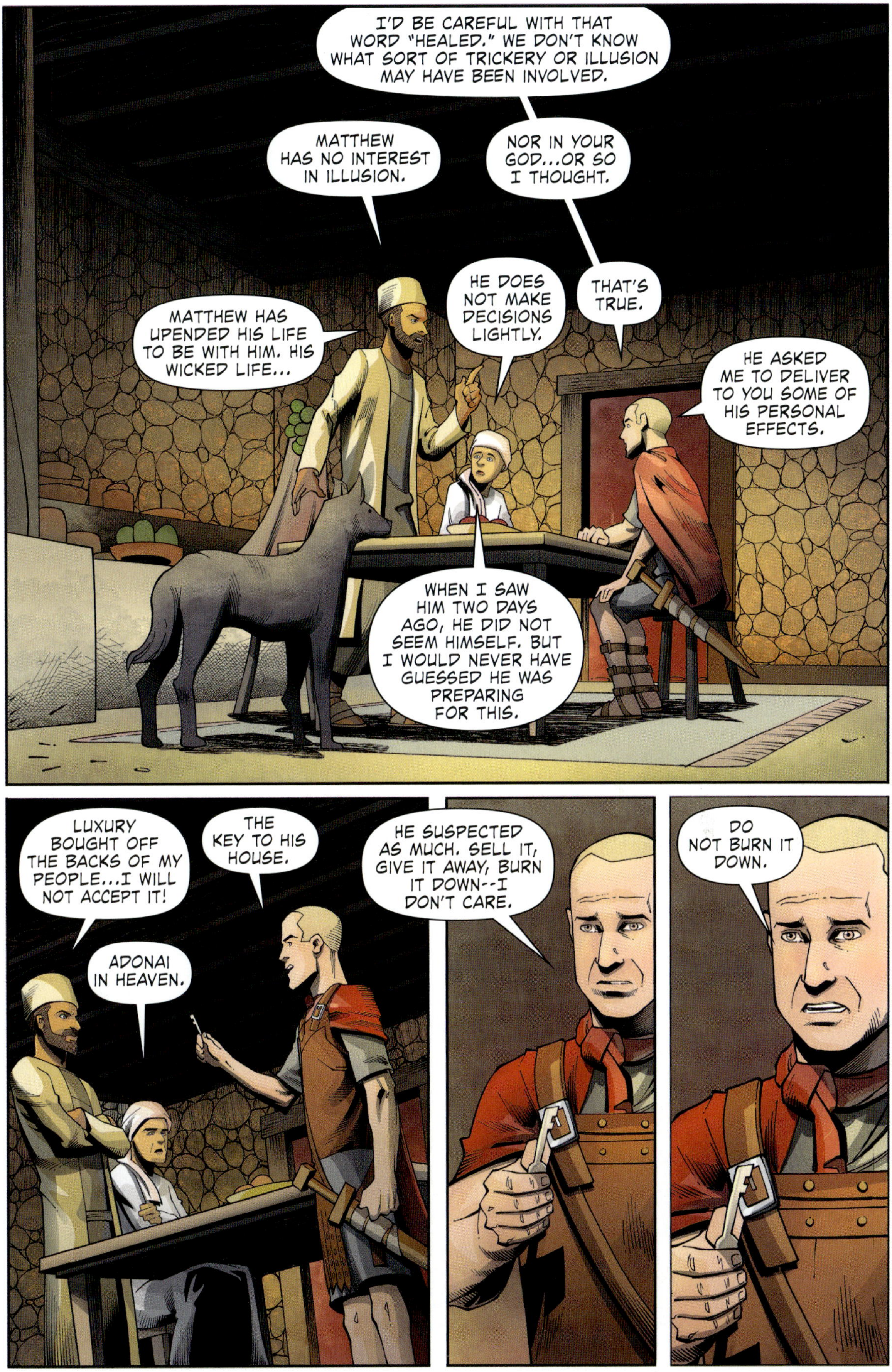

"THIS WAY, MY FRIENDS."

"WE'RE NOT GOING TO THE JORDAN. WE'RE GOING THROUGH SAMARIA."

"ARE YOU TELLING A JOKE?"

"THERE'S A PLACE I WANT TO STOP. PLUS, IT MAKES OUR JOURNEY SHORTER BY ALMOST HALF."

"AND OUR ODDS OF VIOLENT ATTACK MORE LIKELY BY DOUBLE."

"BUT, RABBI, THEY'RE SAMARITANS!"

"THESE WERE THE PEOPLE THAT PROFANED OUR TEMPLE WITH DEAD BONES. THEY HATE US."

"AND WE DESTROYED THEIR TEMPLE ONE HUNDRED YEARS AGO. AND NONE OF YOU WERE PRESENT FOR ANY OF THESE THINGS..."

"WELL, UM...I JUST THOUGHT..."

"GOOD OBSERVATION, BIG JAMES. WHAT'S YOUR POINT?"

"LISTEN, IF WE ARE GOING TO HAVE A QUESTION AND ANSWER SESSION EVERY TIME WE DO SOMETHING YOU ARE NOT USED TO, IT'S GOING TO BE A VERY ANNOYING TIME FOR ALL OF US."

"WE'LL BE FINE."

TROUBLE

TO BE CONTINUED...